D0958563

A.D.

XPLORE THE DEEPER MEANING OF THE BOOK OF ACTS

BASED ON THE EPIC TV SERIES EVENT

NBC

OUTREACH®

Official A.D. *Study & Guidebook*
© 2015 by LightWorkers Media, LLC
Published by Outreach, Inc. under license from Metro-Goldwyn-Mayer Studios Inc.
Photographs used by permission of LightWorkers Media, LLC and NBC.
ShareADTheSeries.com

All rights reserved. No part of this book may be reproduced in any form or by any electronic or mechanical means, including storage and retrieval systems, photocopy, recording, scanning, or other, without permission in writing from the publisher, except by a reviewer who may quote brief passages in a review.
Published by Outreach, Inc. Colorado Springs, CO 80919
www.Outreach.com

Unless otherwise noted, all Scripture quotations are taken from the *Holy Bible, New International Version*® (NIV®). Copyright © 1973, 1978, 1984, 2011 by Biblica, Inc.® Used by permission of Zondervan. All rights reserved worldwide. www.zondervan.com. Other versions used include: the Holy Bible, New Living Translation (NLT), copyright © 1996, 2004, 2007 by Tyndale House Foundation. Used by permission of Tyndale House Publishers, Inc., Carol Stream, Illinois 60188. All rights reserved; the Holy Bible, English Standard Version® (ESV®), copyright © 2001 by Crossway, a publishing ministry of Good News Publishers. All rights reserved; and *The Living Bible* (TLB), copyright © 1971, used by permission of Tyndale House Publishers, Inc., Carol Stream, Illinois 60188. All rights reserved.

ISBN: 9781942027140
Written by Jeremy Jones
Cover Design by Tim Downs
Interior Design by Tim Downs and Alexia Garaventa
Edited by Tia Smith

Printed in the United States of America

CONTENTS

INTRODUCTION: THE *A.D.* EXPERIENCE

Welcome to the *Official* A.D. *Study & Guidebook*, your bridge between the epic TV miniseries *A.D.* and the Bible's book of Acts.

A.D. is a landmark television series event that will reach millions of viewers on NBC beginning Easter Sunday 2015. From the world-renowned producing team of Roma Downey and Mark Burnett, *A.D.* continues where *The Bible* series left off. *A.D.* dives into the world-changing events that followed the crucifixion of Jesus Christ. It brings to life the joy and pain of Jesus's followers as they began to spread His message throughout Jerusalem, across Israel, and eventually around the world—all in a context of political upheaval, persecution, and spiritual revolution.

The powerful drama is based on the Bible's book of Acts. As the weekly episodes of *A.D.* unfold on-screen, small groups or individuals can use the *Official* A.D. *Study & Guidebook* to dig deeper into the biblical text and historical context. The visually stunning depiction brings a new dimension to the deep and rich words of Scripture. Together they point viewers and readers toward the loving Father, the humble and triumphant Son, and the transformative Spirit. The encounter can be life changing.

TAKING ACTION

Most of us know the Bible book by the simple title Acts. In some translations of the Bible, the book is officially named the Acts of the Apostles. It has also been called the Acts of the Holy Spirit. In truth, it's both.

Whichever you call it, Acts is well named. It's a book of stories. It describes the actions taken by the men and women alive during the earliest days of the Christian Church. And it's not too far of a stretch to say its characters were action heroes—not muscle-bound, caped, flying warriors, but ordinary, everyday men and women filled with the miraculous power of the Holy Spirit. The actions they took have reverberated through eternity. Their courageous obedience and faithfulness shaped the Church and did no less than change the world. They made it possible for the incredible message of Jesus to reach you and me today, more than two thousand years later.

What's encouraging is that the real people of Acts were nothing special. In fact, they were probably the last people you or I or any human strategist would have chosen to accomplish much of anything. Yet this was the group entrusted with spreading God's message around the world.

It's true they had walked with the Son of God, sat at His feet, learned from His teaching, witnessed His miracles. So they had this faith thing down, right? Hardly. They still didn't get it. As much as they had learned from Jesus, their perceptions of what the Messiah would do were shaped by their culture, and their vision of worshipping God was rooted in their lifelong Jewish experience. They walked through the trauma of their Master's torture and death with all the perspective, emotions, and grief of humans. The resurrection was met with an equal rush of joy, bewilderment, and new faith.

But the events of the Bible were still unfolding for them moment by moment. They had to live daily. They had to respond, to obey, to move forward even when the path was unclear. They had to act. They had to put their belief and trust into motion one step at a time.

As the book of Acts opens, the apostles are receiving their final instructions from Jesus on earth. The end of His physical presence in their world is only the beginning of their mission. Now comes the test.

What will they do? How will they act? How will we? Jesus's call always requires a response. What will ours be?

Step into *A.D.* Walk with the apostles of Acts. Encounter the life-changing power of God as Father, Son, and Holy Spirit. And never be the same.

HOW TO USE
THIS STUDY AND
GUIDEBOOK

Based on the epic TV series *A.D.*, created by the world-renowned producing team of Roma Downey and Mark Burnett, this study and guidebook is designed to help viewers experience the epic stories of the first followers of Christ taken from the first ten chapters of Acts during the early days of the most powerful global movement in history. It includes powerful lessons from each episode, Scripture readings, and relevant application sections to help you discover the truths for yourself.

The book is designed primarily as a twelve-week small group study guide that can be used for *A.D.* viewing parties, small group studies, or Sunday school classes. However, it can also be used by individuals, and it makes a great follow-up gift for visitors during the Easter season.

Each of the twelve chapters in the book helps readers dig deeper into Acts. Inspired by the themes of each *A.D.* episode, the lessons cover a specific Scripture passage, tie to broader biblical teaching, and provide practical, personal application. Each lesson includes the following sections:

REVIEW

This short recap of each week's *A.D.* episode includes the main action points as a reminder of what took place visually before you launch into the Bible study.

READ

Scripture references from Acts are provided here as the anchor and starting point for each week's episode and study.

KEY VERSE(S)

The key verse or verses from the Bible passage represent the main theme of the study.

REFLECT

This is your chance to dig deeper into the Bible passage and see God's greater work in the book of Acts and beyond. This section draws from the main Scripture and explores the deeper context and meaning of the Bible passage. It blends summary of the biblical account with additional insights into the events and spiritual lessons of the text.

APPLY

As the stories of Acts come to life in new and exciting ways, you may find questions coming up such as:

- "What are we supposed to do with the information we are getting?"
- "How am I to respond to what I've learned?"
- "How should the lessons in Acts impact my life?"

This section addresses those questions with practical tips and personal applications.

DISCUSS

These thoughtful questions are central to the small group study. This is the time for members to personalize the material and application points. And discussing responses offers greater breadth and depth of application for all. The final item in this section of every lesson includes additional Scripture references to encourage your group to go deeper into the Word of God.

PRAY

This written prayer can be read aloud as a group, or it can be used as the beginning or end of a prayer time when group members are encouraged to speak their own prayers.

ACT

This section offers a simple suggestion for how to put the lesson into practice. Consider it a homework assignment for group members. It offers a hands-on way for each individual to put into action what they are learning. Encourage your group members to share with each other what they did during the previous week, how it went, and how it impacted their understanding of Acts.

DID YOU KNOW?

These sidebars in each lesson help to fill in the gaps of context for the readers, sometimes historically, sometimes geographically. They can be used simply as interesting supplemental information or as a launching point for further discussion, research, and discovery.

For more information on leading your group through the *Official A.D. Study & Guidebook*, see the *A.D.* Leader's Guide at the back of this book.

LESSON

1

HOPE FOR A NEW BEGINNING

REVIEW: EPISODE 1

In the aftermath of Jesus's crucifixion, we find His followers unsure of what to do and what to believe. Peter is wracked with guilt over denying and deserting Jesus. He is lost and alone. Judas, Jesus's betrayer, battles his own guilt and tragically takes his own life. Peter finally regroups with other followers of Jesus, John and Mary, but his guilt is only magnified when he discovers that they stayed with Jesus to the bitter end. Faced with the death of Jesus and their own emotional struggles, Jesus's followers question whether they should wait in the city for three days until the promised resurrection or run away.

But Jesus's followers aren't the only ones struggling with the recent events. In the wake of the trial, Caiaphas must face tough questions from his fellow priests, especially Joseph of Arimathea. Joseph questions whether executing Jesus was the right move. Feeling sorry for Jesus and His family, Joseph petitions Pilate to release the body for a proper burial.

By having Jesus's body buried in his own tomb, Joseph has inadvertently fulfilled Isaiah's prophecy that the Messiah would be laid to rest "with the rich"

DID YOU KNOW?

Caiaphas: The Jewish high priest during Jesus's adult life, serving from about AD 18 to 36. He was part of the trial of Jesus and the plot to kill Him. He was a religious leader, subject to the Roman authority of Pilate.

Joseph of Arimathea: A member of the Sanhedrin (Jewish court). He was a wealthy man who requested the body of Jesus after His crucifixion and provided the tomb for burial.

(Isaiah 53:9). Caiaphas is furious. Just when he thought he had the Jesus problem solved, Joseph brings it back to life.

Caiaphas explains to Pilate how allowing Jesus's body to be buried was a mistake. In his attempt to control the situation, Caiaphas convinces Pilate to place soldiers and a Roman seal over the tomb where Jesus is buried. These should prevent the Christians from stealing the corpse and staging a "resurrection." Pilate grants the request, hoping that it brings an end to the whole Jesus episode.

Both temple and Roman guards are in position before the tomb, but they're helpless to stop Jesus from raising Himself from the dead as He had predicted. The guards are terrified when an angel appears and rolls the stone away from the entrance.

The story of Jesus and His disciples isn't over. It is just beginning.

DID YOU KNOW?

Pontius Pilate: Roman governor of Judea from AD 26 to 36. Pilate presided at the trial of Jesus and gave the order for His crucifixion.

READ

Matthew 28:1–20

KEY VERSES

"The angel said to the women, 'Do not be afraid, for I know that you are looking for Jesus, who was crucified. He is not here; he has risen, just as he said. Come and see the place where he lay. Then go quickly and

tell his disciples: "He has risen from the dead and is going ahead of you into Galilee. There you will see him." Now I have told you.'"
—Matthew 28:5–7

REFLECT

Have you ever had your world rocked?

I don't mean bad hair days or even the kind when the Charlie Brown rain cloud seems to hover over your head and follow you around. We all have those. I'm talking about feeling gutted. Destroyed. That hollow, sickening feeling of dread—like your stomach has left your body because the entire earth just dropped out beneath you like a giant trapdoor in the cosmos.

Maybe the feeling was preceded by a statement like one of these:

- "It's cancer . . ."
- "I don't love you anymore . . ."
- "We're letting you go . . ."
- "It isn't you; it's me . . ."
- "I'm sorry. There's nothing else we could do . . ."
- "We regret to inform you . . ."

It's not a place any of us wants to be. In fact, we spend a great deal of energy and effort to avoid being in that place. If you've been there though, you have an idea of what Jesus's followers were feeling. His arrest, torture, and execution rocked their world like nothing else could. Suddenly, their master and teacher was gone. They were left empty, shocked, and grieving in disbelief. They must have felt numb, alone, and afraid.

Can you imagine their confusion? They had left everything and risked everything. They had literally followed Jesus around the country. They trusted Him. They believed in Him. They depended on Him. They didn't always understand, but still they followed His lead, listened to Him, and did what He said. And, oh, the things they had witnessed: events and emotions that defied the very world they lived in. They watched and took part in supernatural experiences—absolute miracles.

DID YOU KNOW?

Writing Acts: Some scholars believe that the Gospel of Luke and the book of Acts were originally written as one work. The form of writings in those days sheds some light on this possibility. Papyrus rolls were used as the "paper" for writing in Jesus's day. These rolls were no more than thirty-three feet long. So literary works during this time were limited to the length of a papyrus roll. Luke's Gospel is the maximum length for a document, and another papyrus roll would have been needed for the book of Acts.

Now what? Jesus was gone. What did it mean? Where were the miracles when Jesus needed them? Was it all a lie or a fantasy? How could Jesus have been so brutally abused and killed? How could He have stood so powerless at the hands of such brutality? If He was the Messiah, how could He be dead?

Jesus's followers were devastated. Their hearts were utterly broken. Their hope was obliterated. This was the end.

Or was it?

A NEW BEGINNING

The Bible's book of Acts is not an isolated story. It describes epic events that laid the foundation for the global Church and shaped the history of the world, but the book itself is a sequel of sorts. It is a continuation of the Gospels and their accounts of the life of Jesus. Acts is the story of the early followers of Christ as they work out the reality of following a crucified, resurrected, and ascended Jesus.

So to enter Acts, we have to look back—just like the author did. Acts opens with this statement by Luke: "In my first book I told you, Theophilus, about everything Jesus began to do and teach until the day he was taken up to heaven after giving his chosen apostles further instructions through the Holy Spirit" (Acts 1:1–2, NLT).

We can't launch into Acts without first understanding where the apostles and early followers were coming from. We must start at the end—the end of sin's reign over humanity and the end of death's power—the crucifixion of the Messiah. It looked like the end of all hope to the disciples. You and I can quickly read and discover that what looked like the end was truly the beginning. But it was three days before the angel declared, "He is not here; he has risen, just as he said" (Matthew 28:6). Those three days were agonizing for Jesus's followers as they tried to come to grips with their grief.

Even though Jesus had talked about these events before His death, His followers did not understand and weren't prepared for the realities they faced. Let's take a closer look at how two different followers responded when life didn't go as they expected.

PETER

Peter was always at the center of things, including Jesus's ministry. He followed Jesus like he lived his life: with passion and reckless abandon. Peter was the disciple who acted first and thought second, and that meant he was no stranger to the taste of his foot in his mouth. But Peter was also in the inner circle of Jesus's disciples, and he witnessed some amazing events.

Shortly before Jesus came to Jerusalem for His final days, He took three disciples with Him and headed up a mountain. There they witnessed the Transfiguration. Jesus changed before their eyes. His face shone like the sun, and His clothes glowed with white light. Moses and Elijah showed up and began to talk with Jesus. As if that weren't enough, the voice of God the Father spoke out loud: "This is my Son, whom I love; with him I am well pleased. Listen to him!" (Matthew 17:5).

DID YOU KNOW?

Simon Peter: One of Jesus's original twelve disciples, Peter's name was given to him by Jesus and means "rock." Originally a fisherman from Galilee, Peter is known for impulsive moments of faith like when he got out of the boat and walked to Jesus on the water. Despite his denial of Jesus three times at His crucifixion, Peter is later forgiven and restored by Jesus and goes on to lead the early church.

Talk about a supernatural experience! Peter, James, and John were completely awestruck. Can you imagine witnessing a miraculous scene like that? What better proof and assurance that Jesus is God's Son could anyone ask for? How could anyone doubt after that?

But they did, especially Peter. The rugged, strong disciple was also plagued with fear. For all his brashness, he was also weak. When things got tough and felt like they were spinning out of control, Peter still denied knowing Jesus three times before His crucifixion—despite all that he knew, had seen, and believed (Luke 22:54–62), despite his claims that he would never desert Jesus (Matthew 26:33).

Peter shows us great moments of faith, but we also see very real fear when faced with the unexpected. To top it off, Peter was overwhelmed with guilt for letting down Jesus. His weakness had been exposed. He had done exactly what he swore he would never do. All his fellow disciples heard Peter boast to Jesus, "Even if everyone else deserts you, I will never desert you" (Matthew 26:33, NLT). Peter must have felt humiliated. While his heart wailed at the loss of his Rabbi, his head screamed reminders that no one deserted his Lord more blatantly and forcefully than he did. How many are the moments that Peter ached to go back and erase! Peter was lost and alone in a dark wilderness of shame. He was a broken man.

MARY MAGDALENE

The Bible gives us few details about Mary Magdalene, but we know her life was transformed by Jesus. Luke 8:2 describes her as "Mary (called Magdalene) from whom seven demons had come out." Whether it was actual possession, mental illness, or a neurological illness such as epilepsy, Mary was set free from her bondage. And her response was wholehearted. She literally followed Jesus like the disciples, most likely caring and providing for them along the way (Luke 8:2–3).

Mary's devotion didn't waver. She stood by Jesus till the end, enduring the horrors of the chanting mobs during Pilate's trial, the beatings of Jesus, and the gruesome procession as He carried the cross to Calvary. Worst of all, she watched with Jesus's mother and John as sneering Roman soldiers raised Him up on the cross and mocked while Jesus suffered until His death. Mary followed all the way to the grave. She stood ready to do whatever she could to comfort her Lord.

As Mary watched the men roll that giant stone across the mouth of Jesus's grave, her broken heart must have screamed with visceral pain. Mary's grief was all consuming and overwhelming. What would happen to her now? Did she even care?

HOPE FOR THE NEW BEGINNING

Three days later, the universe shifted. Eternity was changed. Death was defeated. Jesus secured ultimate victory over evil.

We get to enjoy the vantage point of history. We know the rest of the story. But can you imagine not knowing what would happen next? Can you taste the bewilderment of going to perform a burial ceremony and discovering the body is gone? Would you have trusted your own eyes and ears as they took in an angel saying, "I know you are looking for Jesus, who was crucified. He isn't here! He is risen from the dead, just as he said would happen" (Matthew 28:5–6, NLT)?

Mary Magdalene: Through the years, Mary Magdalene has often become associated with the prostitute who anointed Jesus's feet with perfume and dried them with her hair (Luke 7:36–50). This association with Mary Magdalene gained popularity after the 1300s when the Catholic Church established its first Magdalen House to help reform prostitutes or "fallen women." However, there is no evidence from the Bible or the writings of the early church fathers that suggest Mary was a prostitute or the same woman who anointed Jesus. By contrast, all fourteen biblical references to Mary distinguish her by her hometown, Magdala, a thriving coastal city in Jesus's day. And Luke's introduction of Mary includes her in a list of women who were contributing financially to support and care for Jesus, so she most likely had the means to do so. We do know Jesus had physically, emotionally, and spiritually healed Mary, and she was a leader among followers in her faithful devotion to the Master.

What if one of your closest friends *told* you that's what she had seen?

Can you grasp what a complete contrast the angel's appearance and message were to every single event and emotion of the last three days? No wonder the women at the grave "were very frightened but also filled with great joy" as they went running to deliver the angel's message (Matthew 28:8, NLT). Jesus was alive! Jesus *is* alive! The cross was only the beginning. And this hope for the hopeless made possible by His resurrection is what He still offers to us today.

APPLY

What about us? Where do we turn when our hearts are broken? What do we do when our pain and problems are greater than our worst nightmares? How do we handle our screaming emotions when the events of our lives go spinning out of control and leave us terrified, confused, and broken?

1. Don't deny.

When life truly blows up, it's hard to deny. But even in grief, we often want to escape our pain or pretend it isn't there. Psychology and medicine have demonstrated time and again that ignoring such emotional pain only causes it to fester and grow like a cancer; eventually it will come out in harmful ways. Instead, we have to accept and walk the dark road just as Jesus's followers did.

The good news is that we're not on our own in the process. God knows. He understands. And He wants to comfort us. The Bible is filled with reminders to not be afraid. Jesus Himself said it many times, including, "Do not let your hearts be troubled and do not be afraid" (John 14:27). The words aren't a correction; they're an encouragement. They are a recognition that our natural response as humans is to get scared by what we don't understand and can't make sense of. But they are also an offer of God's supernatural comfort and healing that can lift us out of our deepest fear and pain.

2. Trade the fear.

Or pain, or anger, or doubt, or confusion. God is big enough to handle our emotions. The Psalms are filled with examples of poets, musicians, and writers pouring out their rawest emotions to God. But then what? The process is cathartic, but we must replenish our emotions with something else: God's promises. The Bible is filled with His words of comfort, encouragement, strength, and hope. Meditating on these verses means focusing on them—and refocusing on them again and again to let them replace our pain with the hope of God's promises. Start with John 14:27 or Psalm 34:18, and look up others to serve as medicine for your soul.

3. Do the next thing.

Depending on our circumstances, that might just be breathing, or eating, or getting out of bed. For most of us, it's probably taking the normal steps of life that keep us functioning and connecting with the people who love and care for us. For most of the disciples, it was gathering together as they normally would—at least they wouldn't be alone. For Mary Magdalene and some of the other women, it was caring for Jesus by giving His body a proper burial treatment. In that process, God met them with new hope when they encountered an angel—and then their resurrected Lord.

DISCUSS

Who do you most identify with in this episode? How would you have responded?

What unexpected turns has your life taken? How did you respond? Would you like to respond differently?

Do trust and faith in God help you see things clearly? Or are they what you need when you can't see clearly? Explain your response.

What actions or steps help you trust God in the midst of pain, fear, or the unpredictability of life?

How have you responded to Jesus's death, resurrection, and call to new life?

Read and discuss the verses below. What do they mean? How do they encourage and challenge you?

> "The Lord is close to the brokenhearted and saves those who are crushed in spirit." —Psalm 34:18

> "Trust in the Lord with all your heart and lean not on your own understanding; in all your ways submit to him, and he will make your paths straight." —Proverbs 3:5–6

> "'For my thoughts are not your thoughts, neither are your ways my ways,' declares the LORD. 'As the heavens are higher than the earth, so are my ways higher than your ways and my thoughts than your thoughts.'" —Isaiah 55:8–9

> "Jesus Christ is the same yesterday and today and forever." —Hebrews 13:8

PRAY

God, we acknowledge that you are in control of our lives. Thank you that when things don't go as we expect, you are never surprised. Thank you that where we see an end, you see the beginning of something new. Please reveal to us where, like Jesus's disciples, we've responded to life's circumstances with guilt, uncertainty, doubt, and control. Give us courage to trust. Help us to live out the hope of your new life.

ACT

Go for a walk this week. Every time you come to a corner, stop sign, or stop light, take a minute to think about a time when things didn't go as you expected. See if you can remember how you responded, what it looked like to trust God in the midst of all that was happening, and how He worked (or is still working) in your life through those unexpected circumstances.

LESSON

WAIT FOR IT

REVIEW: EPISODE 2

The news is bad for Caiaphas. When the temple guards inform him about the angel and the open tomb, Caiaphas knows he must act quickly to nip the problem in the bud. He realizes that Pilate hasn't yet heard the news, so he bribes the guards to keep quiet about what they saw. Caiaphas sends his right-hand man, Reuben, on a hunt for the body. He hopes that once the corpse is displayed, all talk of a resurrection will be put to bed. But Reuben can't find a body.

Meanwhile, Mary Magdalene tells Peter and John that the tomb is empty. The disciples are gathered together in fear when the risen Jesus appears to them. And they are immediately overjoyed. Only Thomas misses Jesus's visit, and he struggles to believe that Jesus could really be resurrected. Only when Jesus appears to him personally does he truly believe.

Pilate discovers from his soldiers that the tomb

DID YOU KNOW?

Evidence of the Empty Tomb: From the start, skeptics and opponents tried to explain away Jesus's resurrection. The Jewish leaders bribed the soldiers to spread the rumor that the disciples had stolen Jesus's body. This tactic is one of the greatest evidences of the truth of the resurrection. The easiest way to prove that Jesus was still dead would have been to show His body. But there was no body; there was only an empty grave, opened by moving a massive boulder under the guard of Roman soldiers. The Jews didn't even try to refute the fact that Jesus was gone.

has been ransacked by a supernatural force. And he's furious: at the guards and at Caiaphas for trying to conceal the incident from him. Pilate demands that Caiaphas hand over all information about Jesus's followers so that he can deal with them once and for all. To make doubly sure that news of Jesus's empty tomb doesn't get out, Pilate has all the guards from that night murdered.

The information from Caiaphas leads Pilate to the Christian safe house. Soldiers ransack the house, but the disciples slip out. With help from the zealot Boaz, they make it safely out of Jerusalem and head to Galilee. There they encounter Jesus. Jesus forgives and restores Peter and reveals that Peter's journey is just beginning. The disciples' joy is overflowing. They are encouraged and find new strength.

Finally, Jesus triumphantly ascends to heaven, surrounded by an army of angels. Before He goes, Jesus instructs Peter and the other disciples to fulfill His mission: go make disciples throughout the world. But first, He tells them they must return to Jerusalem and wait for the Holy Spirit.

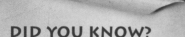

DID YOU KNOW?

Acts's Author: The Bible doesn't specifically name the author of Acts, but Luke is widely accepted as the writer. Besides tradition, here's why: both the Gospel of Luke and the book of Acts begin with similar greetings to Theophilus, and Acts mentions "my former book." Acts overlaps and continues the story of the Gospel of Luke, and the writing styles, themes, and vocabulary match. The writer of Acts also refers to himself as a close companion of Paul, which Luke was.

READ

John 20:1–29; John 21:15–19; Acts 1:1–8

KEY VERSE

"But you will receive power when the Holy Spirit comes on you; and you will be my witnesses in Jerusalem, and in all Judea and Samaria, and to the ends of the earth." —Acts 1:8

REFLECT

Remember that feeling you had as a kid during the Christmas season? You had your sights set on that one extra-special, best-ever-in-the-history-of-the-world toy or gadget. Would it show up under your tree? You shook and shook those colorful boxes, but you just couldn't tell. The big day was coming, but time couldn't tick by fast enough. December seemed like an eternity!

You know the feeling? As you got older, maybe it came as you looked forward to your driver's license, an engagement ring, your wedding day—and night, or your soldier coming home.

We hate that feeling.

• As a culture, we're terrible at waiting. We cook in microwaves… or we pick up fast food—from a drive-through—but if there's a line of cars to sit behind, we explode in road rage. We send instant messages because a ringing phone takes too long. Our blood boils if we have to wait for our YouTube video to download on our smartphone. We spend millions of dollars on gadgets and processes to keep us from waiting.

We've come a long way since the ancient Israelites.

THE LONG WAIT

If the Israelites had to choose a one-word description of their history, *waiting* would have to be high on the list of possibilities. It's not that they liked waiting any more than we do. They hated it too. But their history as individuals and as a nation is full of waiting, especially for the Messiah.

As a people, the Israelites waited to be freed from slavery in Egypt. They waited to enter the Promised Land. They waited for Moses to come down with the Ten Commandments. They waited to get a king. Just to name a few national examples.

The Bible also tells the stories of individual Israelites who did a lot of waiting: Noah, Joseph, Moses, and many more. Abraham and Sarah are one of the most well-known examples of people who waited for God's promise to be fulfilled. God told Abraham that his descendants would outnumber the stars, yet the couple remained childless until Sarah's old age—really old age. Abraham was one hundred, and Sarah was at least ninety years old. (You can read their long story of waiting in Genesis 12–21.) Despite their impatience, doubt, and attempts at taking control of the process, Abraham is honored in the New Testament for his faith and for his waiting: "And so after waiting patiently, Abraham received what was promised" (Hebrews 6:15).

The nation of Israel collectively had also been waiting for thousands of years for the Messiah to come. Prophets prophesied. The nation cycled through phases of being conquered and released. And the people longed for the promised Messiah to come and free them from their oppression.

Finally, after all that waiting, Jesus the Messiah had come. People like Simeon and Anna knew it from the start. They both had spent long lifetimes waiting diligently for the coming of the Messiah and the fulfillment of God's promises. They fasted and prayed and visited the temple daily to worship and seek God's answer of the Messiah. When Mary and Joseph brought Jesus to the temple to dedicate their baby to God, Simeon and Anna recognized Him as the Messiah. They rejoiced and praised God and blessed the baby who had now fulfilled their greatest expectations (Luke 2:25–38).

The waiting was over! Wasn't it? Jesus's followers had thought so. They believed He was the Messiah, the Son of God. But then: the unthinkable, the nightmare, the crucifixion—and all their dreams seemed dashed. They spent three days trying to sort it all out, to make some sense of Jesus's death and what they would do now.

Two of Jesus's followers said it well in Luke 24:21: "We had hoped he was the

DID YOU KNOW?

Kingdom Expectations: Jesus's followers often had different ideas about the Messiah than what Jesus taught. And those expectations were alive even after the resurrection. They still didn't completely get it. Acts 1:6 tells us, "So when the apostles were with Jesus, they kept asking him, 'Lord, has the time come for you to free Israel and restore our kingdom?'" (NLT). As God's chosen people, the people of Israel expected the Messiah to bring about a political state and power for world domination. The Jews looked forward to God intervening in world history to free them from their oppressors—the Romans in Jesus's day—and to give them the world sovereignty they'd never known. Instead, Jesus brought a spiritual kingdom founded on love, not political power.

Messiah who had come to rescue Israel" (NLT). Notice the past tense. That was right before Jesus revealed Himself to those two as they walked together along the road to Emmaus. The men hit the road right back to Jerusalem to tell the disciples that it was true: Jesus *was* alive!

Hope reignited. It had begun when Mary Magdalene discovered the empty tomb and heard Jesus speaking her name as He stood in front of her (John 20:16). It spread when Jesus appeared in the room where the disciples were gathered behind locked doors. Jesus was back! And He began a series of appearances to His followers over the next forty days. During that time, Jesus brought clarity to their confusion, and He gave them instructions: "Do not leave Jerusalem, but wait for the gift my Father promised, which you have heard me speak about" (Acts 1:4).

Seriously? Hadn't they waited enough?

MEETING OUR NEEDS

The disciples didn't seem to mind. They didn't question the waiting. There's good reason why not. Before Jesus asked them to wait, He first met their needs. And His interactions with His followers show us a pattern: provision and promise before petition. In other words, Jesus took care of them, spelled out a promise of what He would do, and then asked something of them.

We see through both Thomas and Peter the way Jesus tenderly provides for the needs of His followers. Doubting Thomas, as he is often called, gets a bad rap. His friends and fellow believers saw Jesus and gave him the report. But without firsthand experience, Thomas struggled to believe.

Did Jesus punish Thomas or make him suffer? No, Jesus specifically let Thomas see and touch His scars so that Thomas's doubt could be replaced with belief (John 20:24–29). Jesus didn't have to provide Thomas with assurance, but He provided it anyway.

Later, Jesus took care of Peter's heart. While some of the disciples were fishing on the Sea of Galilee, Jesus showed up and provided a huge catch. Once they got back on shore to eat some of their bounty, Jesus talked to Peter. "Do you love me?" Jesus asked Peter—three times. There's a question for each time Peter disowned

Jesus. The process reinstated Peter, and Jesus affirmed him three times (John 21:15–17). It's exactly what Peter needed to let go of his shame and find renewed forgiveness and confidence.

• Jesus's example shows His ability and willingness to take care of His followers. And next He gave them a promise: soon they would receive the gift of the Holy Spirit. Only then did He petition His followers: stay in Jerusalem and wait.

APPLY

Despite our culture of instant gratification, we aren't exempt from waiting today. We wait for many temporary things in this life. We also wait for things of eternal value. Like the disciples, we wait for Jesus's return to earth to complete His work—as God's Word promises in Acts 1:11. And as the disciples discovered, God is faithful in giving us provision and promise before petition.

As we follow God through this process, we can find hope in biblical encouragement to wait on the Lord, such as Psalm 27:13–14: "I remain confident of this: I will see the goodness of the LORD in the land of the living. Wait for the LORD; be strong and take heart and wait for the LORD." But what does that look like? And how do we do it?

The waiting process is not simply an absence of activity—it's a realignment of the right activities to allow God's Spirit to change our hearts and minds. Waiting is more active than it initially sounds. Here are several steps to pursue in the process.

1. Be still.

Time to be still is hard to come by in our culture, and that makes doing so all the more necessary and valuable. But we must proactively make time to quiet our minds and environments, to rest, to listen for God's voice in His Word and in our hearts, and to be renewed. "Be still, and know that I am God," says Psalm 46:10. We must prioritize the time to completely focus on God and who He is. Reading the Bible tunes our frequency to God's voice. Repeating a memorized verse holds our focus. And writing prayers can quiet the internal chatter of our busy brains. As we still our bodies and spirits, God shapes and renews us in His time.

2. Expect and prepare.

Waiting on the Lord is an active process of preparation, not a passive lack of action. Think of a pregnant woman. While she waits for her baby to be born, she gets ready because she knows the event is coming. In fact, we often say a pregnant woman is expecting. Similarly, we expect God to work, and we act with faith, preparing our hearts to follow His lead in His time. We seek and obey His Word, knowing that He has clarified instructions for all believers, such as actively loving others and making disciples. As we do, we can expectantly watch for Him to open specific doors in our personal lives.

3. Worship.

Worship transforms us and places our attention and praise on God, where it belongs. We see that's what the disciples did: they gathered together to pray and worship and encourage each other (Luke 24:53). Our worship can take those forms. We can worship through music, but we can also worship with an attitude of offering to God everything we do, no matter how daily the task (1 Corinthians 10:31).

DISCUSS

On a scale of 1 to 10, how good are you at waiting? Why?

Describe a time, past or present, when God asked you to wait on Him. How was it challenging? What was the reward? What did you learn in the process?

As followers of Jesus, we are called to wait for His second coming. Are you tuned in to this waiting? What does it look like in your daily life?

Is waiting on the Lord a more passive or active process? Explain. What helps you to actively wait on God?

Read and discuss the following verses. How are they real in your life?

> "But if we hope for what we do not yet have, we wait for it patiently." —Romans 8:25

"I keep my eyes always on the LORD. With him at my right hand, I will not be shaken. Therefore my heart is glad and my tongue rejoices; my body also will rest secure, because you will not abandon me to the realm of the dead, nor will you let your faithful one see decay. You make known to me the path of life; you will fill me with joy in your presence, with eternal pleasures at your right hand." —Psalm 16:8–11

"I am weary with my crying out; my throat is parched. My eyes grow dim with waiting for my God." —Psalm 69:3, ESV

"I wait for the LORD, my whole being waits, and in his word I put my hope. I wait for the Lord more than watchmen wait for the morning, more than watchmen wait for the morning." —Psalm 130:5–6

"But they that wait upon the Lord shall renew their strength. They shall mount up with wings like eagles; they shall run and not be weary; they shall walk and not faint." —Isaiah 40:31, TLB

PRAY

Heavenly Father, reveal our deepest doubts and our anxious desires to make things happen. Forgive us for our impatient and demanding ways. Thank you that in your grace you provide for our needs. Fill us with your strength and patience as you shape us and guide us in your perfect timing.

ACT

Write down one thing you are waiting for, or one area of your life in which you feel God has told you to wait. Then list one specific, active thing you can do to turn your focus off yourself in your waiting. For example, are you waiting on a new job? Write a letter of encouragement to a friend who is struggling with their work. Are you waiting for physical health? Visit a friend, coworker, or fellow church member in the hospital. Waiting on reassurance in doubt? Find an encouraging, thought-provoking book to read, and invite a friend to read it with you. What are you waiting for?

LESSON

3

PENTECOST POWER

REVIEW: EPISODE 3

As Jesus instructed, the disciples leave Galilee for Jerusalem. The masses are arriving in Jerusalem for Pentecost, including Herod Antipas and his entourage, who have also come down from Galilee.

Caiaphas oversees the fallout from the deaths of six temple priests. Leah thinks people will realize the Romans were responsible for the deaths and worries that it could cause a riot during Pentecost. Making matters worse, during a feast Antipas inadvertently goads Pilate into attending the festival himself. A storm is brewing that Caiaphas will barely be able to avert.

Also traveling from Galilee is Peter's daughter, Maya. Her presence reminds Peter of all he has sacrificed for his mission. But Peter is galvanized when the Holy Spirit arrives—just as Jesus promised. The Spirit transforms Peter and the believers and gives them courage to preach openly in the temple. More than three

DID YOU KNOW?

Pentecost: The harvest festival, or Feast of Weeks, that takes place fifty days after Passover was called Shavuot in Hebrew. It was one of the three major feasts in the Jewish calendar, along with Passover and the Feast of Tabernacles. People traveled to Jerusalem to present an offering of bread at the temple and to commemorate God's gift of the Ten Commandments to Moses on Mount Sinai following the Israelites' escape from Egypt.

thousand place their faith in Jesus at Peter's first sermon. And the message of Christ upstages all the spectacle of Pentecost.

Peter and John follow up their preaching with the miraculous healing of a lame beggar, Melek. In the process, they inadvertently thwart an attempted assassination on Pilate by Boaz, a political zealot. Instead of Pilate, it's a Roman centurion who gets killed. Things are boiling over in Jerusalem.

READ

Acts 2:1–4, 14–15, 38–42; 3:1–11

KEY VERSES

"When the day of Pentecost came, they were all together in one place. Suddenly a sound like the blowing of a violent wind came from heaven and filled the whole house where they were sitting. They saw what seemed to be tongues of fire that separated and came to rest on each of them. All of them were filled with the Holy Spirit and began to speak in other tongues as the Spirit enabled them."
—Acts 2:1–4

REFLECT

Have you ever seen the wind?

Impossible, right? But you've seen the effects of the wind.

Have you ever endured a hurricane? You've at least seen video of meteorologists struggling not to be blown over while roofs peel off the tops of buildings. You've probably seen once-towering trees pushed over to the ground with tangles of roots exposed to the sky. You know what the wind can do.

And everyone has felt the wind. You've bundled up and braced yourself against the sting of an arctic winter blast. You've welcomed the warmth of the breeze signaling the arrival of spring. And you may have enjoyed the soothing caress of a tropical trade wind holding your beachside air to the perfect temperature.

The currents and movement in the air around us are a force of nature that affects us all. We know the wind is real. We've all witnessed its power.

God's Spirit is the same, moving and working in and around us in unseen ways with clear and undeniable results. As God fulfilled His promise to the believers waiting in Jerusalem, we see an unleashing of the Holy Spirit's power in and among Jesus's followers and on the evangelistic work that Jesus called them to before He ascended to heaven. This baptism with the Holy Spirit was visible, powerful, and undeniable.

SEEING THE SPIRIT

As the book of Acts opens, there was a lot going on in Jerusalem as the disciples gathered to wait just as Jesus had instructed. Jews from miles around came to Jerusalem during this time to worship and sacrifice in celebration of the Feast of Weeks, or Pentecost. This year, the atmosphere was especially charged with religious and political tension in the aftermath of Jesus's crucifixion and as word of His resurrection spread.

As all of this swirled around them, 120 of Jesus's followers gathered on the day of Pentecost. Suddenly, a sound like a roaring wind surrounded them. Flames of fire became visible in the air and rested over them. And they began to speak supernaturally.

The Holy Spirit unleashed His power and filled the disciples in an undeniable way. And when the believers experienced His power, their reaction was not to stay hidden inside or to sit around talking about how amazing it was. Instead, they took immediate action to use God's power for His purpose. They poured outside to share the heavenly message. Some of the crowd there mocked them and said they were drunk. Others, many foreigners, marveled to hear and understand their own language.

Peter clarified that no, they had not been drinking. He quoted from the prophet Joel about this miraculous event they were witnessing. He continued to proclaim that Jesus had indeed risen from the dead to offer forgiveness and new life to anyone who would believe. The message pierced the people's hearts, and three thousand believed. Not only were Peter and the disciples transformed with new power that day, the Church was officially born.

Pentecost is often called the coming of the Holy Spirit. Clearly the Holy Spirit did come in power in a special way, but it is good to remember that as the third person of the Trinity, the Holy Spirit is eternal. God's Spirit had been working throughout history to reveal truth to and through prophets and believers. But the events of Pentecost do mark a time when the Holy Spirit became central to the early church, and His presence was a reality in believers' everyday lives.

Before He left earth, Jesus promised the disciples that they would receive power when the Spirit came to them and that they would be His witnesses throughout the world (Acts 1:8). And His promise reveals His purpose. The arrival of the Holy Spirit was not simply to display power and create excitement but to further the message of Jesus and bring people to faith.

The purpose of the Holy Spirit in our lives and the world today remains the same. The Spirit is the expression of God that is present on earth. His main roles are to bring understanding of Jesus's teaching, to glorify God, and to work in the lives of individuals and the Church. Some of the ways He does so are by enabling humans to confess that Jesus is Lord (1 Corinthians 12:3), providing a variety of spiritual gifts to the body of Christ (1 Corinthians 12:4–27), interceding for us at our deepest levels (Romans 8:26–27), and revealing God's truth (1 Corinthians 2:10–12; Ephesians 3:3–5). He is called the Comforter, the Advocate, and the Helper.

In Acts, as the Spirit begins to work centrally in the new church, we see three main marks of His power in the early believers: truth boldly proclaimed, miraculous signs and healings, and unified community.

All of these signs are present at the baptism of the Holy Spirit in Jerusalem, and they continue after that. We see them manifested in the Acts accounts, including the story of Peter and John healing a disabled beggar (Acts 3:1–11). This man had never walked in his whole life. His healing was incredible and nothing short of miraculous, and the man's response was beautiful. Not only did he get up and walk, he went leaping and praising God throughout the temple. His gratitude and joy were uncontainable. The people around were amazed by this miracle, and that gave Peter the opportunity to tell about the source of this power.

Peter spoke boldly to everyone around, crediting God and proclaiming the message of Jesus. So much for the Jewish leaders silencing the disciples—but they did arrest Peter and John. It didn't seem to faze the disciples; when they were questioned by the Sanhedrin, Peter and John spoke out, clearly proclaiming Jesus as the Christ who brings salvation.

What a transformation in Peter! The fear and shame that plagued him in the past were nowhere to be seen. Now he was boldly taking every opportunity to tell about Jesus.

Peter was definitely at the forefront, but he was not the only one empowered by God. Acts 4:29–31 describes the prayer of many followers who were filled with the Holy Spirit, and it says they spoke the Word of God boldly too.

The great unity within this group of early believers is another clear mark of the Holy Spirit. Acts 4:32–33 describes how the believers formed community and shared their possessions. They didn't even claim them as their own—everything was available to meet the needs of all. It sounds utopian, doesn't it? Of course, these believers were still human, and later in Acts we read about some of the divisions the community faced. But the lesson here remains about caring for our community of believers.

There's one other evidence of the Holy Spirit's work worth noting. The believers prayed, "They did what your power and will had decided beforehand should happen" (Acts 4:28). It wasn't too long ago that, holding onto their political aspirations for the Messiah, they had asked Jesus when He would get busy and set up a political kingdom (Acts 1:6). Now they get it. The Holy Spirit had brought them understanding and a deeper perspective of God's greater work in eternity.

And that is exactly His point. The coming of the Holy Spirit emphasized the fullness of God's triune purposes and power. His goal wasn't to create super-believers who could flex their spiritual muscles, but to transform His followers from the inside out and empower them to draw other people into a healing and redemptive relationship with God.

As the early believers focused on and aligned themselves with those purposes through the power of the Holy Spirit, they experienced great success. As they obeyed and joined in the Spirit's work, proclaiming Jesus and bringing healing and living in unity, they were part of more and more people being restored to God through Jesus—even people who had never seen Jesus.

This is the same Spirit who fills us today for the same purposes.

APPLY

Wow, what it must have been like to be alive at that time! The atmosphere of being part of such a powerful work of God must have been electric. But we can't forget that the believers faced great challenges and persecution too. They also had daily lives to lead as well. In many ways, the earliest days of the Church weren't all *that* different from our own. And regardless of the exact circumstances, the Holy Spirit is still the ever-present expression of God who fulfills and enables God's greater work within and through us. When we strive to do even good things in our own power apart from Him, the results are often failure, frustration, and fear. But when we rely on the power of God's Spirit, peace, power, and God's perspective can prevail. Here are some steps we can take in and through the Holy Spirit.

1. Tune in.

The apostle Paul wrote, "Those who live according to the flesh have their minds set on what the flesh desires; but those who live in accordance with the Spirit have their minds set on what the Spirit desires" (Romans 8:5). Where is our attention? What is our mindset? What do we fill ourselves with on a daily basis? We can think of the Holy Spirit as the essence of God, the experience of God as we live in relationship with Him on earth. But we must turn our minds and focus our hearts toward meeting the Spirit in God's greater work and exercising the gifts He gives us (1 Corinthians 12–14). We must seek His guidance and listen for direction (John 16:13–15).

2. Be bold.

We're all a lot like Peter. On our own, our best attempts are inconsistent and often bumbling, and our weaknesses and fears can debilitate us. But through God's Spirit, we can experience transformation and strength that we never had. We can be used by God in supernatural ways. Zechariah 4:6 is an insightful reminder worthy of our meditation: "'Not by might nor by power, but by my Spirit,' says the LORD Almighty." As we pray and fill ourselves with God's Word, we draw power and confidence from the Holy Spirit, and we can step out boldly and fearlessly as He guides us (2 Corinthians 3:17).

3. Embrace community.

Just as God Himself is a community, our service to Him must be lived out in community. We need the support, encouragement, and accountability of fellow believers. We all still have our flaws just like the early believers, but also like them, we can experience grace and unity through the Holy Spirit (Hebrews 10:24–25; Acts 4:32–35).

DISCUSS

Jesus often seems more tangible to us because He walked on earth as one of us. How do you think of or view the Holy Spirit?

How have you experienced the Holy Spirit in your own life? Describe a time when the Spirit has enabled you to accomplish something unexpected.

How is the early church like or different from our churches today? Explain your reasons.

What's the point of God's power in our lives? Christians hold different views about how the Holy Spirit's power is shown through us today. How can we find unity in emphasizing the *why* (or purpose) of God's power over the *what* in our churches and communities?

Read and discuss the following verses. What do they tell us about the work of the Holy Spirit in our lives?

"For the Spirit God gave us does not make us timid, but gives us power, love and self-discipline." —2 Timothy 1:7

"But the fruit of the Spirit is love, joy, peace, forbearance, kindness, goodness, faithfulness, gentleness and self-control. Against such things there is no law." —Galatians 5:22–23

"There are different kinds of gifts, but the same Spirit distributes them. There are different kinds of service, but the same Lord. There are different kinds of working, but in all of them and in everyone it is the same God at work. Now to each one the manifestation of the Spirit is given for the common good." —1 Corinthians 12:4–7

"In the same way, the Spirit helps us in our weakness. We do not know what we ought to pray for, but the Spirit himself intercedes for us through wordless groans. And he who searches our hearts knows the mind of the Spirit, because the Spirit intercedes for God's people in accordance with the will of God."
—Romans 8:26–27

"The Spirit searches all things, even the deep things of God. For who knows a person's thoughts except their own spirit within them? In the same way no one knows the thoughts of God except the Spirit of God. What we have received is not the spirit of the world, but the Spirit who is from God, so that we may understand what God has freely given us." —1 Corinthians 2:10–12

PRAY

Holy Spirit, please fill us with your presence and power. Lead us into greater understanding of the Father's ways and equip us to accomplish His works. Give us courage and humility to use the power you give for your purposes.

ACT

Worship through music. We do it collectively in church, but what about personally? Combine your personal prayer and Bible study time with worshipping in song. Music has a powerful ability to unlock our emotions and engage our spirits. It provides a focused channel to praise God and prepares our hearts to hear His guidance. If you are musical, play your own instrument. If not, listen to recordings. Either way, try writing your own worship song—lyrics or music. Ask the Holy Spirit to meet you in the process and to lead you to connection with the Father. Invite God to use music as a means of drawing you into His greater purposes in the world.

LESSON

WHAT MATTERS MOST

REVIEW: EPISODE 4

Turmoil and unrest continue to build in Jerusalem. Pilate begins executing civilians in a brutal response to the assassination attempt on his life. He is determined to flush out the assassin and tasks Caiaphas with the job of delivering a suspect named Boaz. The high priest is at a loss for how to stem the executions, which are growing by the day. The political tension rises, and pressure on his position mounts.

Meanwhile, Peter and John are arrested following the tumult they caused at the temple by healing a lame man and preaching the resurrection of Jesus. They prepare themselves for what seems inevitable death as Leah manipulates the healed man, Melek, to say during their trial that the miracle was faked. But in the trial, Melek verifies that he was truly and miraculously healed. The gathered crowd backs the disciples, and the situation forces a frustrated Caiaphas to release Peter and John.

The two disciples immediately go back to work addressing the Christians who have grown in number and are now beyond counting. Among the new converts are a wealthy couple named Ananias and Sapphira and a bold young man named Stephen, who is eager to start preaching in the temple. Barnabas also joins the movement and donates valuable land to the growing church.

Things take a sudden turn for the worse, however, when the Christians are rocked by God's striking down Ananias and Sapphira for lying. It leaves Peter perplexed by this new kind of violent power from the Holy Spirit. The entire movement is deeply frightened. Meanwhile, Boaz and other political zealots attempt to recruit the converted Christians for their own violent revolution against Rome.

Jerusalem is erupting into war with itself.

DID YOU KNOW?

The Supernatural: Acts tells of many miracles and supernatural events, including physical healings. These amazed the people, but they were not isolated to Christianity. The ancient world believed in spiritual realities. Pagans too witnessed miracles and prophecies at the shrines of other gods, perhaps through demonic activity, psychedelics, or other means. So to the first-century church, the supernatural was not necessarily unusual. It was, however, respected and an important part of the believers' testimony to the power of Jesus and the Holy Spirit in their lives.

READ

Acts 4:1–31; 5:11–16

KEY VERSE

"As for us, we cannot help speaking about what we have seen and heard."
—Acts 4:20

REFLECT

When is the last time you threw a rock in a pond? If you have young kids, it's probably been pretty recently. Don't you love the ripples? They can be beautiful and mesmerizing if you take the time to watch closely—or look at one of those professional, close-up photographs. They're also scientifically cool: waves of energy spreading out evenly.

You can't stop them, those ripples. Try it. You might be able to dam one side or section. Then you'll get a backlash as the energy in that water sloshes back against itself. Meanwhile, ripples will continue to roll in every other direction.

There was a similar scenario going on in Jerusalem. It was as if Jesus were a rock in a pond. His death and resurrection sent a ripple effect throughout eternity, impacting everything that ever was, is, and will be. And as those ripples rolled through Jerusalem, the religious and political leaders were scrambling to dam them up. That was impossible. God's restorative work could not be stopped, but the backwash was beginning. And it would cause trouble.

In the middle of it all was the growing group of believers, led by former fishermen and tax collectors, who were changing the world as God's Spirit changed them.

When Peter and John healed the lame man at the temple and preached about Jesus's resurrection, they caused a huge commotion in the crowded center of Jewish life. People were astounded by the miracle and the message. But the priests arrested Peter and John.

In the eyes of the religious rulers, this Jesus thing was a snowballing problem that just wouldn't go away. They had viewed Jesus as a blasphemer and a threat when He was alive, and they thought killing Jesus would be the end of His followers and popularity among the common people. They wanted the movement to stop. Instead, it was growing.

The Jewish rulers had a dilemma on their hands. The Jewish people were praising God for the miraculous healing, and the disciples were leading more and more people to Jesus. "'What should we do with these men?' they asked each other. 'We can't deny that they have performed a miraculous sign, and everybody in Jerusalem knows about it'" (Acts 4:16, NLT).

As Peter and John spent a night in jail, they knew the Sanhedrin held their lives in its hands. This group was the supreme court of the Jews, made up of its top religious leaders and prestigious men. They had turned Jesus over to Pilate and goaded the Roman ruler into crucifying Him.

While that fact would have terrified the disciples not long before, it didn't

DID YOU KNOW?

Sanhedrin: The supreme court of the Jews. Under Roman rule, the Sanhedrin had power, but it could not pass a death sentence unless a Gentile trespassed the inner courts of the temple. The ruling group consisted of seventy-one members. The high priest was in charge. There were priests, mostly Sadducees, who were generally elitists and wanted to maintain the temple traditions; Pharisees, who were fanatical about the law, especially in oral traditions that didn't depend on the temple; scribes, who were experts in traditional law; and elders, who were retired priests and other respected leaders. Collectively, the members of the Sanhedrin were the wealthiest, most powerful, and most intellectual Jews in the land.

DID YOU KNOW?

Disciple or Apostle?: Jesus chose twelve men to follow Him, and they were called the disciples. These men were the students of Jesus during His ministry on earth. The word *disciple* means "a follower and student of a mentor or teacher." While a disciple is a student—one who learns from a teacher—an apostle is sent to deliver those teachings to others. *Apostle* means "messenger." The apostles were the early followers of Jesus sent out to spread the teachings of Christ. Once the Holy Spirit came upon the disciples in Acts 2, they were empowered to follow Christ's call to "Go into all the world" (Mark 16:15) and became known as apostles (no longer just students, but messengers of the good news). The apostle Paul, although he wasn't one of the original twelve disciples, was also referred to as an apostle: "Paul, a servant of Christ Jesus, called to be an apostle and set apart for the gospel of God" (Romans 1:1).

seem to faze them a bit. When the priests questioned them, they didn't hold back. "Do you want to know how he was healed? Let me clearly state to all of you and to all the people of Israel that he was healed by the powerful name of Jesus Christ the Nazarene, the man you crucified but whom God raised from the dead," Peter told them (Acts 4:9–10, NLT).

The rulers were amazed by the disciples' boldness. In the religious world of the Jews, Peter and John were nobodies. Before Jesus called them to be His disciples, they were both workingmen: fishermen throwing and hauling nets on the Sea of Galilee. They had no formal religious training, but the leaders couldn't deny their miraculous work and confident teaching of the Scriptures.

The Sanhedrin absolutely did not want Peter and John to continue, but they couldn't very well stop them either. The best they could do was release the disciples and tell them to stay quiet and stop teaching in the name of Jesus.

That wasn't even an option for Peter and James, and they readily said so: "Which is right in God's eyes: to listen to you, or to him? You be the judges! As for us, we cannot help speaking about what we have seen and heard" (Acts 4:19–20). And that's exactly what they kept doing.

It's clear that Peter and John had plugged into a new power source. Fueled by the strength of the Holy Spirit, they were fearless.

TRUTH AND TRANSPARENCY

What did send fear through the disciples and the church were the deaths of Ananias and Sapphira.

This wealthy couple belonged to the church. As the believers shared generously to care for each other, a man named Barnabas sold some land and gave the money to the apostles. Maybe Ananias and Sapphira liked the attention he got or maybe the Holy Spirit prompted them to do the same. Whatever the motivation, the two sold some real estate and brought the money to the apostles to be used in support of the community of believers.

But they didn't give all the money. They made it look like they were giving everything, when in fact they were keeping some for themselves. When Peter confronted each of them separately, it was clear they were still trying to cover up the truth. But their dishonesty wasn't hidden from God, and Ananias and Sapphira were struck dead.

The church and everyone who heard about their deaths were terrified. So far the believers had seen the power of God's Spirit used for miracles and healing, filling people with strength

DID YOU KNOW?

Barnabas: Born Joseph, he was given the name Barnabas when he joined the apostles in Jerusalem and gave his possessions to the community of believers there. The name Barnabas means "son of encouragement." Barnabas was a mentor for Paul after his conversion and went with Paul on his first missionary journey.

and courage, and bringing peace and unity. Suddenly, God's power was unleashed for judgment, destruction, and death. The event had a huge impact on the believers. Is this what happened when they sinned? After all, everyone knew that they weren't perfect. Could this happen to them?

This story in Acts is a difficult one, and our natural reaction is probably similar to the ancient believers'. The harshness of the judgment against Ananias and Sapphira was and is hard to reconcile with a loving, forgiving God. There is no question the couple was at fault, but their punishment seems frightfully severe. And why did they receive death when others didn't?

We don't know exactly. Their deaths were another sign that God is present and active among His people, and they served as a reminder to the early church, and to us, that while God is merciful and full of grace, He does not tolerate sin. When Peter rebuked the couple, he pointed out that they weren't just lying to the church leaders, they were lying to God and testing His Spirit.

In a broader context, maybe striking down these two was an act of protection by God for the early church. Selfishness and deceit had no place in the community of believers. Instead of leaving it to grow and damage the church from the inside out, God removed it quickly.

Despite the pain and fear that this event brought, more and more people believed in Jesus and joined the church body (Acts 5:14). God's power had been seen in a new way, but it had not changed. It was still bringing miraculous healings, salvation, and hope to those who believed (Acts 5:14–16). And even in the face of opposition and fear, the early church still grew.

APPLY

When things got tough, the disciples persevered because they knew what mattered most. They weren't afraid of men. Their reverence, awe, and love for God were much stronger. They knew that God's power and plans were far greater than any obstacles humans could throw in their way. They also knew that God expected their obedience, and they trusted that He had better plans and purposes in mind even when they didn't fully understand His ways. Surely, even the leading apostles must have felt fear sometimes, but they relied on the Holy Spirit's strength to act with courage. Here are several important applications we can take away from their example and the events in Acts 4–5.

1. Please God, not man.

We like to fit in. We like to be liked. But we all face pressure from people around us that runs opposite of God's ways. Our culture encourages us in blatant and subtle ways to live for ourselves rather than Jesus. Who should we listen to and obey? That was no contest for Peter and John. They are an excellent example that the Holy Spirit gives us the strength and courage we need to keep God first and to follow His voice. We should have the same attitude as the psalmist: "The LORD is with me; I will not be afraid. What can mere mortals do to me?" (Psalm 118:6). At the same time, we should keep a sense of reverence and awe for God as we respect and pursue holiness through the power of His Spirit (Proverbs 19:23; Matthew 10:28).

2. Prioritize prayer.

The first thing the believers did once Peter and John were released by the Sanhedrin was gather in prayer. They praised and thanked God for the disciples' safe release, and they asked for continuing strength and boldness (Acts 4:24–30). The early believers spent a lot of time praying. Prayer is the lifeline that realigns our hearts and spirits to God's. It's our way to communicate with Him, and as we do, He reshapes us and gives us what He knows we need: strength, courage, comfort, guidance, assurance, and more. To know God's heart and grow into who He wants us to be, we must keep in touch with Him.

3. Be real.

The fact that the story of Ananias and Sapphira is included in the Bible shows us that God values brutal honesty. The story is not a pretty picture. It shows flaws in the early church from the start. It also shows what God thinks of hypocrisy and lies. At the same time, there were a million other sins going on that God didn't punish with death. We can be encouraged that God would rather have our humble honesty, even when it's not pretty. As we lay our weaknesses before God, we find forgiveness through Jesus and can allow the Holy Spirit to change us from within. As Paul wrote in 2 Corinthians 12:9, God's power is made perfect in our weakness, and His grace is enough to take care of us.

DISCUSS

If you were arrested for following Jesus, what would you do?

What is the attitude of our culture toward living for Christ? What pressures or limitations do you face? How do you deal with them?

How do you picture or view God? What do you think shapes that view? How can you let God shape your understanding of His character?

What has God done or what is He doing in your life that you can't help speaking about? How do you let other people know about the work God is doing in your life?

Read and discuss the following verses. How do they encourage and help us to pursue transparency with God and fellow Christians?

> "When you are brought before synagogues, rulers and authorities, do not worry about how you will defend yourselves or what you will say, for the Holy Spirit will teach you at that time what you should say." —Luke 12:11–12

> "The fear of the LORD is the beginning of knowledge, but fools despise wisdom and instruction." —Proverbs 1:7

> "I hate all your show and pretense—the hypocrisy of your religious festivals and solemn assemblies. I will not accept your burnt offerings and grain offerings. I won't even notice all your choice peace offerings. Away with your noisy hymns of praise! I will not listen to the music of your harps. Instead, I want to see a mighty flood of justice, an endless river of righteous living." —Amos 5:21–24, NLT

"Devote yourselves to prayer, being watchful and thankful."
—Colossians 4:2

"If we confess our sins, he is faithful and just and will forgive us our sins and purify us from all unrighteousness." —1 John 1:9

PRAY

Heavenly Father, we praise and respect you because you are bigger and greater than we can fully comprehend. Thank you for your grace and mercy in our lives. Thank you for drawing us near to you and tenderly re-creating us. Continue reshaping our hearts. Give us the strength and courage to live transparently with you and others. And let your Spirit flow through us to reflect you with humble confidence and bold honesty.

ACT

* Come clean and quit hiding. Write an honest assessment of your heart to God. It's okay, God already knows; but there is healing in confession and transparency. Ask the Holy Spirit to guide you. Write some strengths as well as weaknesses. Plan to shred your paper when you're done—it will give you more freedom to not worry that someone will see what you've written. Offer your letter to God. You may also want or need to talk with someone after you're done to confess, pray together in accountability, or ask for help to take steps toward change that the Holy Spirit reveals in this process.

LESSON

A BIGGER PICTURE

REVIEW: EPISODE 5

Claudia is increasingly disgusted by Pilate's brutality against Jerusalem's civilians, but he ignores her pleas to call off the daily executions. So Claudia meets with Leah to form an unlikely partnership to help bring the killings to an end.

Among the believers, Peter is having problems that arise from the unwelcome distraction of the zealot Boaz. Many followers are now terrified of Peter after the deaths of Ananias and Sapphira. Having people afraid of him is a new and unsettling experience for Peter, and he has to draw upon the strength of his daughter, Maya. Peter is also distracted by Stephen's fiery desire to preach at the temple.

Boaz is increasingly wracked with guilt over the civilians suffering in his name. Against the advice of the Thin Man, he gives himself up to Caiaphas, who in turn passes him on to Pilate. But Boaz has eaten poison, thus robbing Pilate of his chance to inflict countless tortures. Pilate is so incensed that he goes back on his agreement with Caiaphas and proceeds with the day's crucifixions anyway.

— different than series

Boaz's body is grotesquely displayed in public, and the apostles are among the gathering crowd. They continue to spread their popular message, but as they stir up the crowd, they're arrested by the temple guards. An angel releases them from jail. But instead of going underground, Peter and John immediately go back to the temple courts and continue their preaching. Caiaphas has them arrested once more and tried immediately.

This time the apostles are saved by the wise figure of Gamaliel, who angers Caiaphas by calling for clemency. Instead of the death penalty, the apostles are whipped publically. The scene is morbid. Stephen is among the watching crowd, and he is disgusted by what he sees. Stephen finally preaches his sermon, and the crowd rises up in anger against him.

The mob seizes Stephen and stones him. God does not rescue Stephen but lets him be martyred. Holding the cloaks of those doing the stoning is the incomprehensibly vicious Saul.

READ

Acts 5:17–41; 6:8; 7:1–8:1

KEY VERSES

"But Stephen, full of the Holy Spirit, looked up to heaven and saw the glory of God, and Jesus standing at the right hand of God. 'Look,' he said, 'I see heaven open and the Son of Man standing at the right hand of God.'" —Acts 7:55–56

REFLECT

Do you remember those popular hidden pictures from the 1990s? You know, the ones with a repeated pattern all over them—anything from jelly beans to animals to paisleys to actual photographs of your favorite movie characters. If you stared long enough or in the right way, a *different* 3-D image would appear and look like it was floating. Back then, they were everywhere.

Husbands would hold them up to wives and ask, "Do you see it?" Girlfriends would point and ask boyfriends, "Do you see it now?" Brothers would jeer, "Ha, ha, you can't see it!"

"Can too," sisters would shout back. "Oooh, it's a unicorn!"

Or a cat or a car or a palm tree. There was no end to the images that could suddenly float off the page (or the wall—it was cool to frame them).

The trick was all in how you looked at the picture. If you focused on the obvious pattern, that's all you would see. You had to adjust your vision—kind of scale back your eyes and let them go out of focus. Then *aha!* there it was.

In Acts, there was a lot going on that could have easily obscured the believers' vision of God's bigger picture. Peter and John were arrested again—it seemed to be becoming a habit. This time the high council decided to kill them, but a Pharisee named Gamaliel persuaded the council to flog Peter and John instead. It was still a brutal punishment. The cost of following Jesus was rapidly rising. These threats, pressures, and punishments were growing worse all the time.

All the Christians knew what was at stake. All of them were in danger. They met publicly in the temple to worship and preach about Jesus. All of them would have been known to the priests and Jewish leaders. They certainly must have felt fear and asked, "What have we gotten ourselves into?" They must have felt their vision blur in and out from the threats in front of them to the bigger picture of God's work beyond. But Peter and John immediately returned to preaching in the temple: "Jesus is the Messiah" (Acts 5:41–42).

DID YOU KNOW?

Gamaliel: A respected and beloved Pharisee, known as a kind and tolerant man. The Pharisees generally believed that while God was sovereign over all things, man had freedom and responsibility for his actions. When the leaders wanted to kill Peter and James, Gamaliel argued that they should be careful not to go against God. If the work among the apostles was not of God, it would fade like other attempted revolutions.

STEPHEN SEES MORE

Stephen was another leader in the new church who saw the bigger picture—past, present, and future. He was "a man full of God's grace and power, [who] performed great wonders and signs among the people" (Acts 6:8). And he was definitely driven by a passion for something much greater than his own life.

When Stephen was arrested, he recounted the history of the Israelites through the stories of Abraham, Joseph, and Moses. He highlighted the Jewish fathers' obedience to answer God's call and venture out, not stay comfortable and privileged. Abraham obeyed and went to an unknown land when God said, "Go." He waited on God's promise of many descendants even into his old age. Joseph didn't understand the bigger picture until years after his brothers sold him into slavery, but all through the injustices, he was faithful to serve God as he watched a bigger story unfold. Then there was Moses, who traded his life of power and status in Egypt to lead the Israelites out of slavery and to the edge of the Promised Land.

What truly incensed the Jewish leaders was that Stephen suggested they had limited God and become legalistically enslaved to the temple instead of truly obeying God: "The Most High does not live in houses made by human hands" (Acts 7:48). Even more, Stephen didn't mince words when he accused the religious leaders of killing the Messiah: "Was there ever a prophet your ancestors did not persecute? They even killed those who predicted the coming of the Righteous One. And now you have betrayed and murdered him" (Acts 7:52).

It was the last straw. The leaders went ballistic. They dragged Stephen to the edge of town to stone him. All the while, Stephen kept his focus beyond the chaos before him and on God's bigger picture—literally. He saw a vision of the eternal and described Jesus standing at God's right hand (Acts 7:55–56). As Stephen died, he followed Jesus's example and prayed for God to forgive his murderers (Acts 7:59–60).

Stephen had known the risks that speaking the truth held, but he boldly spoke God's truth anyway. His knowledge of and focus on God's bigger story gave him the strength and courage to forgive those who could only see and act on the immediate. Even when it was clear that Stephen's own story was ending, he kept his gaze on eternity.

We have the privilege of seeing even more of God's bigger story through

DID YOU KNOW?

The Seven: At the beginning, all the early Christians in Jerusalem were Jews, but there were divisions among the Jews. The Jerusalem and Palestinian Jews spoke Aramaic and Hebrew and considered themselves purer Jews. The Hellenist Jews lived beyond Palestine or were Gentiles who had converted to Judaism; they spoke Greek. The Christians followed the long Jewish tradition of caring for the sick, orphans, and widows. But the Hellenists claimed they weren't getting equal treatment. So the apostles chose seven leaders to take care of problems like this in the church community. Stephen was one of these men.

His Word. We can trace the stories of other individuals who looked beyond their immediate troubles to follow God into His bigger purposes—Mary and Joseph, Jesus Himself, Peter, John, and Paul, just to name a few. In fact, the Bible gives us a glimpse of God's bigger picture for the spread of the Gospel when it mentions that Saul was present and approved of Stephen's stoning. At the time, no one could imagine Saul's future involvement in God's unfolding story.

APPLY

When we look at immediate events and problems, things often don't make sense. In this Acts account, why were Peter and the apostles rescued multiple times but Stephen stoned? In our world and lives, we ask, "Why, God?" about so many different pains, problems, and tragedies. Our struggles, decisions, and to-do lists loom large and obscure our field of vision. They close in on us, calling for our attention, and the more we fixate on them, the easier it is to lose the bigger picture beyond.

Thankfully, God is still writing a bigger story in our individual lives and in eternity around us. When its plot twists seem unpredictable, He calls us to look to Him. When we can't see beyond our pain, He has promised to provide us what we need. His Spirit can change our vision, reshape our focus, and provide a clarity that defies whatever struggles loom before us. We can trust that there is a bigger story at work in the world, written by a God of love and redemption.

Here are some steps we can take to find clearer vision.

1. Look at what God has already done.
The Bible's example of God's work in individual lives and in human history turns our attention to His greater work and His loving care for us. Living life among fellow Christians brings encouragement of His work all around us as well as support to keep up hope. Both can be a "great cloud of witnesses" to carry us through (Hebrews 12:1–3). And sometimes we need to look back and remember God's specific faithfulness in our own lives. He has helped and taken care of us in the past; He will do it again.

2. Choose forgiveness.

Stephen surrendered without anger—just forgiveness. Forgiving others brings freedom for us and even opens the door for us to be forgiven (Mark 11:25; Luke 6:37). Jesus taught us to "love your enemies and pray for those who persecute you" (Matthew 5:44). Wow, that can be hard! But as the Holy Spirit gives us strength to do so, we are transformed, and we can transform others with action that is so completely different from the world around us.

3. Focus on the eternal.

We know how God's story will end. We know that Jesus won the ultimate victory over sin and death, and we know that His work isn't done. He will come again to finish making everything right (1 Thessalonians 4:16–17; Revelation 19:11–16). And we can trust that in the meantime He is working out His greater purposes for our good (Romans 8:28). Reading God's Word helps to bring His big picture into focus and offers hope that defies our immediate problems. He will fill us with strength to stand strong like Stephen, knowing that there is eventual, ultimate victory beyond whatever we face.

DISCUSS

What practical steps help you to remember and focus on God's bigger picture? Are there any beyond the normal spiritual disciples (such as exercising, talking to a friend, writing, drawing, etc.)?

When have you been able to deal with hardship because you had a view of something greater?

Is there any area of your life where you need to stand for truth? What if you risked negative consequences? What about death?

Who do you need to forgive? How might that open the door to recognizing God's greater work in your life?

Read and discuss the following verses. What do they tell you about God's bigger story in the world and in your life?

> "'For my thoughts are not your thoughts, neither are your ways my ways,' declares the LORD. 'As the heavens are higher than

the earth, so are my ways higher than your ways and my thoughts than your thoughts.'" —Isaiah 55:8–9

"Therefore we do not lose heart. Though outwardly we are wasting away, yet inwardly we are being renewed day by day. For our light and momentary troubles are achieving for us an eternal glory that far outweighs them all. So we fix our eyes not on what is seen, but on what is unseen, since what is seen is temporary, but what is unseen is eternal." —2 Corinthians 4:16–18

"And we know that in all things God works for the good of those who love him, who have been called according to his purpose." —Romans 8:28

"For now we see only a reflection as in a mirror; then we shall see face to face. Now I know in part; then I shall know fully, even as I am fully known." —1 Corinthians 13:12

"Blessed is the one who perseveres under trial because, having stood the test, that person will receive the crown of life that the Lord has promised to those who love him." —James 1:12

PRAY

God, please reveal the areas where we can't see the eternal because we are so focused on the immediate. Take our troubles and pain; we don't know how to solve them alone. Let your Spirit use them to teach us, shape us, and use us. Give us a bigger vision for your bigger, eternal picture.

ACT

Prayerfully take time to edit your story. What problem are you facing? What experience has led you into pain? For each of the next three or four days, spend fifteen minutes writing about it. Write honestly and explore your emotions freely. Explore how you would like to see God use this experience to shape you or change the ending. Zoom out from this struggle and consider how this chapter might fit in the bigger context of your life, your family, human history, and God's eternity.

LESSON

SCATTERED SEEDS

REVIEW: EPISODE 6

The daily executions by Pilate have stopped, and attention returns to the threat caused by the growing Christian community. Caiaphas is under increasing pressure to take care of it at all costs while Annas fears that Caiaphas has made himself so unpopular that the role of high priest may actually pass to another family. He attempts a coup to replace Caiaphas with his son, Jonathan. Antipas agrees to back Jonathan, but Pilate foils the plot.

Stephen's martyrdom has unnerved the Christian community. As Stephen is buried, Saul begins his persecution against the Christians in fury.

Peter feels some responsibility for Stephen's death, but aided by the Holy Spirit, he finds the strength to preach in Jerusalem. Saul decides to arrest those who are caught listening to the apostles' preaching. Yet still the Christian numbers grow. Ultimately, Saul is forced to take even more extreme measures. He joins up with Caiaphas, who sanctions the use of brutal violence to beat the Christians into compliance.

Saul exacts his punishment upon the Christians by burning down their commune. The Christians are scattered, yet they preach as they go. It becomes apparent that the only match for Saul's brutality is their courage and belief.

READ

Acts 8:1–4; Acts 26:9–11; Galatians 1:13

KEY VERSE

"Those who had been scattered preached the word wherever they went." —Acts 8:4

REFLECT

What happens when you don't exercise? One day you look in the mirror and realize your muscles have shrunk! The rest of you has probably grown, mostly around the middle.

If you've ever had an arm or leg in a cast, you know firsthand that when muscles aren't used, they atrophy. When muscles aren't stretched, tested, and used, they gradually waste away. If you've ever done any kind of weight lifting or resistance training, you know that the breakdown and rebuilding of muscle tissue is what makes it grow bigger and stronger.

The same is true for our spiritual growth—even though we don't like that fact. It's also true for the life of the Church as a body of believers. In Acts, we see the seemingly impossible growth of the early church at the same time that it is being challenged and tested most.

DID YOU KNOW?

Destruction: The word used in the Greek, *elymaineto*, to describe Saul's persecution of the church is a term used to describe a wild boar ravaging a vineyard or a wild animal savaging a body. The word choice makes it clear that Saul's actions were ones of extreme brutality and cruelty toward the believers. The depth of his hatred and cruelty toward Christians makes the story of his later conversion and his role in spreading the Gospel all the more powerful.

WITH A VENGEANCE

Once Stephen was killed, widespread persecution was unleashed on the believers. And no one was a more ferocious persecutor than Saul of Tarsus. Saul was a man on a mission: to do everything he could to oppose Jesus and destroy the early collection of His followers. Even he later said so in Acts 26:9–11 and Galatians 1:13.

Saul's methods were brutal, and his means were intense. Not only did he arrest those speaking in public, but he went house to house dragging out Christians and throwing them in prison. He testified against believers, put them in prison, beat them, had them killed, and even hunted them down in foreign cities. He was essentially the Jewish leaders' most ferocious enforcer.

Why was Saul so harsh? Later chapters in Acts and the letters he wrote give us insights into Saul's early life. Saul was a Pharisee, and he was adamantly devoted to the law. He had a strong Jewish pedigree; his ancestors were Pharisees (Acts 23:6). He had grown up in the important port city of Tarsus, where he probably received a strong general education, along with a strong education in the Scriptures (Acts 26:4). But even that wasn't enough for Saul. He came to Jerusalem to study deeper, and he was rising through the ranks of religious leaders (Galatians 1:14). Saul was wholeheartedly devoted to God, and he longed for a pure Israel that strictly and completely adhered to God's laws. From Saul's perspective, Jesus and His followers blasphemed God and God's laws. He saw these Jews as an offense to God, and he was willing to purge them before they corrupted Israel any more.

Oh, the irony! Little did Saul know about God's bigger picture, and that God was already using him to strengthen and spread the message of Jesus.

Faced with the threat of torture and death, believers naturally fled Jerusalem. As the believers scattered, Christianity spread and grew beyond Jerusalem to Judea, Galilee, and Samaria, and even beyond the borders of Israel around the Mediterranean and Asia Minor. It was the beginning of the fulfillment of Jesus's statement at the beginning of Acts: "But you will receive power when the Holy Spirit comes on you; and you will be my witnesses in Jerusalem, and in all Judea and Samaria, and to the ends of the earth" (Acts 1:8). The early church faced persecution, fear, and scattering, but instead of weakening, it grew in numbers.

Credit these early believers for showing courage and faithfulness. Once they moved to safety, they didn't just hide or abandon their new faith. They continued meeting together to worship, and they proclaimed Jesus in local synagogues, taking the message farther and farther. As they continued to work out what it meant daily to follow "the Way," as they called it (Acts 9:2), they shaped Christianity beyond the Jewish ways back in Jerusalem.

The twelve apostles showed incredible courage and stayed in Jerusalem. Their worship practices were rooted in their Jewish traditions and directed toward Jews. The apostles knew that Jesus was the Messiah, and they were still coming to understand that He had been sent for the entire world. For the time being, they focused their ministry activities on the center of the Jewish world, even when it put them in great danger.

Persecution didn't stop with Saul. As we'll see later, it grew worse for the early church. It has continued throughout history and still exists today around the world. Yet wherever Satan has attempted to stamp out the flame of Jesus's followers, sparks and embers have continued to glow. Even out of the most evil atrocities, God is able to bring healing and restoration.

DID YOU KNOW?

Persecution: In the earliest days of the Church, persecution came from the Jews. The Romans would join in soon enough and take the oppression to new levels of brutality. Yet even in the Roman Empire, persecution was not a constant experience for Christians. And it was not always empire-wide. Instead, it was sporadic and localized, spaced sometimes by long periods of relative tranquility. The first long peace for Christians lasted from 211 to 250 (briefly interrupted in 235), and the second from 258 to 303. It is estimated that more people have been martyred for Christ in the past fifty years than in the Church's first three hundred years.

APPLY

Thankfully, most of us live where we enjoy freedom of religion. Our religious liberties are under attack at times, but for the most part, we don't face the threat of physical persecution and death. That is something to be deeply grateful for! But our sense of comfort can lead to complacency if we let it. Unless we are disciplined to exercise our faith—both personally and collectively—it shrinks like muscles that are never worked out.

By contrast, there are things in our culture that challenge our faith, such as relativism, fear of rejection, or our own questions and doubts. When we face them head-on instead of trying to avoid them, we create opportunities for our faith to grow. And when we do so as a body of believers, we create opportunities for people outside the walls of the church to hear the good news of Jesus and believe.

So what should your spiritual workout include? Here are a few steps you can take to exercise your spiritual muscles.

1. Know what you believe.

Jesus said, "Love the Lord your God with all your heart and with all your soul and with all your mind" (Matthew 22:37). Notice the part about the *mind*. Much of the opposition we face today comes from philosophies that attack or try to dismiss our faith. But there is a great deal of evidence in support of the truth of the Bible. Apologetics is the practice of studying and making a case for the truth of the Christian faith.

Start by reading some books on the subject (try *The Case for Christ* by Lee Strobel, *More Than a Carpenter* by Josh McDowell, or *On Guard* by William Lane Craig). Join a class or small group. Learn, practice, and prepare how to engage others in real conversations about the questions and complexities of faith and to explain them with confidence.

2. Look for opportunities—everywhere.

It wasn't choice that spread the early church beyond Jerusalem—it was unimaginable hardship. But even then, the believers "preached the word wherever they went" (Acts 8:4). There may be tough situations in your life that you'd never choose. Maybe you are spending hours in a hospital because a parent, child, spouse, or friend is sick. Or maybe the loss of a job has sent you to work somewhere you never would have chosen just to make ends meet. Whatever the situation, look for opportunities to share the love of Christ with people you meet. When you are pushed outside your comfort zone, look for the chance to bring the love, hope, and good news of Jesus into that place.

3. Seek support.

Find other people with a similar desire to live for Christ. Share life with them; support each other. Knowing you are not alone can bring encouragement, hope, and confidence to continue faithfully growing in and sharing your faith. Maybe you are now in a position to give support. Look for someone who needs to lean on you. This may be literal support through money, food, service, or conversation. And it may also be encouragement, prayer, and a spiritual example to stay focused on God's bigger picture.

DISCUSS

Are your spiritual muscles fit or flabby? Honestly assess your spiritual health and what has contributed to it.

We live in a culture that values and emphasizes comfort. How does that cultural outlook impact your spiritual view? How does it affect your willingness to share about Jesus? What would you do differently if you knew someone wanted to kill you because of your beliefs?

Describe a time when hardship brought about deeper connection or growth. In what ways?

How are you supporting and being supported by others in your faith right now?

Read and discuss the following verses. What do they tell you about using every life experience as an opportunity to share Christ?

> "For I am not ashamed of the gospel, because it is the power of God that brings salvation to everyone who believes: first to the Jew, then to the Gentile." —Romans 1:16

> "Sing to the LORD, praise his name; proclaim his salvation day after day. Declare his glory among the nations, his marvelous deeds among all peoples." —Psalm 96:2–3

> "But in your hearts revere Christ as Lord. Always be prepared to give an answer to everyone who asks you to give the reason for the hope that you have. But do this with gentleness and respect." —1 Peter 3:15

> "Religion that God our Father accepts as pure and faultless is this: to look after orphans and widows in their distress and to keep oneself from being polluted by the world." —James 1:27

"The weapons we fight with are not the weapons of the world. On the contrary, they have divine power to demolish strongholds. We demolish arguments and every pretension that sets itself up against the knowledge of God, and we take captive every thought to make it obedient to Christ." —2 Corinthians 10:4–5

PRAY

God, forgive us for our complacency and addiction to comfort. Please fill us with the strength and boldness of your Spirit. Reveal opportunities to spread your Word. Protect your people around the world. Please keep them safe and strong, and use your Church in mighty ways.

ACT

Today, 322 Christians are killed for their faith each month, according to Open Doors. These are our brothers and sisters. Pray for them and the persecuted church. Get a map; put a pin in a country; lift up in prayer the people there. (Voice of the Martyrs has an online prayer map.) Keep praying through different countries. Visit Voice of the Martyrs (persecution.com) and Open Doors (opendoorsusa.org) to learn about ways to support fellow Christians around the world who are in danger because of their faith.

LESSON
7

A WIDER CIRCLE

REVIEW: EPISODE 7

Saul continues his persecution of the remaining Christians. His focus: to find Peter at all costs. The apostles are forced into hiding. Many others flee Saul's thugs. Mary Magdalene takes a job working in Pilate's palace, to gain money and supplies to support the church. In the palace, she meets Joanna, an old friend and fellow Christian from Galilee, who is married to Chuza, household manager to Antipas.

Of all the scattering Christians, Philip has uncanny bravery. He goes to the poor, violent province of Samaria, whose people have not seen eye to eye with the Judeans for centuries. Philip is beaten by bandits but then slowly starts to win over the Samarians with miracles and healings. Even the local leader, Simon the Sorcerer, an initial rival to Philip, believes and is baptized in the name of Jesus.

Pilate and Claudia hear big news: Emperor Tiberius is coming to Jerusalem as part of his tour of the provinces. Pilate is determined to make a good impression so Tiberius will promote him to the much bigger job of governor of Syria. That would finally get him and Claudia out of Jerusalem.

DID YOU KNOW?

Tiberius: When the Gospels refer to Caesar, it is Tiberius they are talking about. He was the Roman emperor from AD 14 to 37. Many important biblical events took place during his reign, including the beginning of John the Baptist's preaching; Jesus's ministry, crucifixion, and resurrection; Stephen's martyrdom; and Paul's conversion. Tiberius was known to have a difficult personal life marred by multiple marriages and divorces. However, he was a successful military leader throughout his reign.

Pilate tells Caiaphas that as part of his cleanup of the city, he wants all persecution and arrests of Christians to stop. He doesn't want the emperor thinking things are out of control. Caiaphas instructs Saul to halt the arrests. Saul agrees but then continues anyway.

The emperor arrives with his entourage, including two young men, Caligula and Herod Agrippa. They are corrupt and dangerous and instantly make a bad impression on Pilate and Claudia. Pilate tells Caiaphas that Saul's renewed persecutions are putting at risk his own promotion. Caiaphas has to get rid of Saul for good, so he sends him out to Damascus.

READ

Acts 8:5–25

KEY VERSE

"Philip went down to a city in Samaria and proclaimed the Messiah there." —Acts 8:5

REFLECT

We've all done it. We've all taken one look at someone and made up our mind about them. We've judged another person unfairly.

We preach, "Don't judge a book by its cover." But we practice, "You only get one chance to make a first impression." And our snap judgments come cold, harsh, and fast.

Sometimes, we don't even give people the benefit of a chance to make a first impression. We automatically lump them into our categories based on the neighborhood they live in, the job they do, the school they attend, the church they worship in, the party they vote for, the color of their skin, or the region or country they came from. We might say we don't have anything against them, but we're fine to keep our distance and let them keep theirs, thank you very much.

But have you ever had that encounter with another person when all your preconceptions got turned upside down? Maybe that "thug" helped you on the roadside. Maybe the "transient" offered the spare change you were missing in the checkout lane. Maybe one of "them" was the only person to offer encouragement. Maybe "that guy" (or girl) you hated at first impression ended up becoming your best friend. Maybe "they" were nothing like you'd been told.

If any of these scenarios sounds familiar, you've had a taste of the feelings between Jews and Samaritans.

FAMILY FEUD

Back in the early church, the political drama and religious persecution continued to grow. Like Stephen, Philip was one of the Seven, the officers chosen by the apostles to help settle disputes among the believers (Acts 6:1–6). The easiest and safest thing for Philip would have been to hide out. But Philip made a different choice. He did decide to get out of Jerusalem, but it wasn't to save his skin—it was to spread the good news about Jesus to Samaria.

DID YOU KNOW?

Samaria: The mountainous central region of ancient Palestine was established as the biblical northern kingdom of Israel. Samaria was the capital city of the kingdom of Israel. In biblical times, Samaria reached from the Mediterranean Sea to the Jordan Valley. Today it is generally known as part of the West Bank.

This was a bold choice. Samaria was a region long known for its violence and poverty. Even more, there was a long history of animosity between the Jews and Samaritans. They hated each other.

The hostilities between these two peoples had been running for hundreds of years. It all got started after King Solomon's death, when Israel divided into the northern and southern kingdoms. Samaria was the capital of the northern kingdom, which was called Israel. And Jerusalem was the capital of Judah, the southern kingdom. Both kingdoms disobeyed God and turned from His ways. And eventually both kingdoms fell to invaders and were ruled by other empires: the Assyrians, Egyptians, and Babylonians.

Once the invaders took over, most of the Jewish people were scattered or taken away to live in captivity. Those in Israel intermarried and blended their cultural and religious beliefs and customs with those of the foreigners, the Assyrians. Many Assyrians also adopted the Jewish religion and worshipped Yahweh. The Samaritans were the descendants of the mixed races.

When the Jews in the southern kingdom were conquered by the Babylonians, they were taken into captivity but allowed to live together. And they maintained their spiritual and cultural traditions and Jewish identity. When they were allowed to return to their own land under Nehemiah's leadership, the Samaritans offered to help them rebuild the walls of Jerusalem (Ezra 4:1–2). But the southern Jews said no. They didn't trust the Samaritans and didn't want any help from a corrupted and idolatrous people.

The Samaritans built their own temple at Mount Gerizim to worship there instead of in Jerusalem. To the Judeans, this was counterfeit worship and unacceptable in God's eyes. That divide never went away (John 4:20).

The animosity continued in the New Testament. Both groups excluded the other with restrictions on entering places of worship, marriage, and any kind of social relations. Jews looked down on Samaritans and treated them as Gentiles. There was great separation and hatred between the groups.

Jesus Himself broke through the barriers. When He met the woman at the well in John 4 and asked for water, she was surprised He was even talking to her. Jews just didn't associate with Samaritans. Jesus told her the time was coming when true worshippers would worship in spirit and truth, not only at the temple and not separated as Jews and Samaritans (John 4:21–23).

So when Philip went to Samaria, he was following Jesus's lead. He was going to those who were rejected with a message that the Jews didn't think they deserved. Hatred and distrust went both ways, and the Samaritans were likely skeptical of Philip at first. They didn't need another Jew telling them they were wrong in how they worshipped God. But Philip was offering Jesus's good news of love and forgiveness equally to all people. Philip brought healing, miracles, and joy to the people, and many of them believed in Jesus. Even the prominent Samaritan figure Simon the Sorcerer chose to follow Jesus—though Peter and John had to help Simon see that God's gift and the power of His Spirit could not be bought or controlled. <u>A people marginalized, judged, and excluded was now brought into the center of God's grace through Jesus.</u>

When Peter and John heard what was happening, they immediately went to Samaria and prayed for the believers there to receive the Holy Spirit. By doing this, they completed the inclusion. They didn't question the authenticity of Samaritan faith. They didn't grumble and ask Philip what he thought he was doing taking Jesus's message to "those" people. Instead, the church leaders included and supported the new believers.

DID YOU KNOW?

Not for Sale: When the Samaritan Simon the Sorcerer saw the power of the Holy Spirit, he wanted it. He offered money to Peter and John to get the power to give the Holy Spirit to others, but they rebuked him (Acts 8:20–23). The gift of salvation through Jesus and the power of the Holy Spirit are gifts of grace, not things that can be bought, used, or controlled. The term *simony* still means "the buying or selling of church offices or favors."

APPLY

Our world is full of divisions. <u>But we are called to go to the Samaritans in our lives and break down barriers.</u> It's easy for us to be pulled into our biases, even in our efforts to pursue and please God. Because of that, we have to be all the more purposeful in extending love and grace to people outside our automatically positive perceptions. Instead of bunkering behind the walls of "us" and "them," we are to widen the circle of Christ's love to others. How do we do so?

1. Look to the edges.
It's what Jesus always did. He sought and saw the beggars, sinners, tax collectors, women, and children—<u>all the people on the margins or outside Jewish religious life.</u> He proclaimed that He had brought

good news for the poor and freedom for the prisoners (Luke 4:18). He said, "I have not come to call the righteous, but sinners to repentance" (Luke 5:32). We are the ones who need Jesus's forgiveness, and we are the ones called to bring His love to the world, including the hurting, broken people around us. Looking at our actions, who do we really believe Jesus's message is for?

2. Listen.

In order for relationship to exist, there must be give and take. And in order to bridge deep divides, there must be a willingness to listen to the experiences or hurts of the other person. A good doctor listens to a patient's concerns before prescribing medicine. A friend listens instead of doing all the talking. Jesus gave us the example in His interaction with the Samaritan woman (John 4:1–26). He gave her a chance to speak, and He listened. Who is crying for help around us? Who is lashing out from hurt? We must reach out with a loving hand and listening ear.

3. Build unity.

For us, it's not usually the person from the radically different culture on the other side of the world who is hardest to love. More often, our more difficult challenge is with the neighbor, family member, or coworker whose skin color, language, rituals, values, ancestry, history, or customs are different from our own. It's those people we are called to love. Yet our churches are too often known by the differences between them instead of our unity in following Jesus. Our socioeconomic classes separate us physically and relationally. And racial wounds run deep in our nation. It takes a conscious choice and deliberate effort to acknowledge and reach across the divides. It takes humility, patience, and willingness to listen and serve. Take the first step by reaching out in your neighborhood, workplace, or community. Talk with your church leaders about what you can do collectively to love the "others" around you.

DISCUSS

Who do you find it hardest to love and include?

Where do you see a need for unity in your church and community? In your state and nation?

Have you seen someone or some group that is good at including the outcasts? What characteristics stood out to you?

How can you be part of widening the circle of your church to include those who are currently on the outside?

Read and discuss the following verses. What do they tell you about the inclusive nature of the good news of Jesus and our role in sharing it with all people?

> "For God did not send his Son into the world to condemn the world, but to save the world through him." —John 3:17

> "Therefore, as God's chosen people, holy and dearly loved, clothe yourselves with compassion, kindness, humility, gentleness and patience. Bear with each other and forgive one another if any of you has a grievance against someone. Forgive as the Lord forgave you. And over all these virtues put on love, which binds them all together in perfect unity." —Colossians 3:12–14

> "Live such good lives among the pagans that, though they accuse you of doing wrong, they may see your good deeds and glorify God on the day he visits us." —1 Peter 2:12

> "Live in harmony with one another. Do not be proud, but be willing to associate with people of low position. Do not be conceited." —Romans 12:16

> "So in Christ Jesus you are all children of God through faith, for all of you who were baptized into Christ have clothed yourselves with Christ. There is neither Jew nor Gentile, neither slave nor free, nor is there male and female, for you are all one in Christ Jesus." —Galatians 3:26–28

PRAY

Heavenly Father, reveal where we have a limited view of your salvation. Show us our prejudices and misperceptions and lead us beyond them. Help us to embrace those on the outside with open arms and the good news of Jesus's love. Widen our hearts with your grace and love, and widen our circles of influence as we offer that love and grace to others.

ACT

Build a bridge—or repair one. Is there someone you have a strained relationship with? Maybe a person from another class, tradition, race, or religion? Invite them to have coffee, take a walk, or share a meal. Let love and getting to know them be your only agenda.

LESSON

RESPOND
TO GOD

REVIEW: EPISODE 8

Under pressure from Pilate, Caiaphas is eager for peace in the city during Tiberius's visit and convinces Saul to leave Jerusalem under the pretense that Peter has gone to Damascus. Saul gathers his men and heads to Syria, accompanied by Reuben. On the way, Saul encounters the risen Jesus and is blinded.

With Tiberius in Jerusalem, Pilate begins his bid for the position of Syrian governor. But the young brats Caligula and Agrippa anger everyone with their debauchery, and when Pilate loses his cool, he threatens Caligula's life. Claudia bonds well with Tiberius, and he promises a return to Rome for her and Pilate soon.

Peter and John come out of hiding while Saul is gone to Damascus, and they go join Philip in Samaria. Here Peter meets Simon the Sorcerer, who tries to buy the Holy Spirit from him. Peter's anger almost results in Simon's death by God, but his fervent prayer and repentance save him.

In Pilate's palace, Claudia is having bad dreams, but Pilate is too focused on his promotion to pay them any attention. He promises to nominate Antipas as his successor, as long as Antipas takes Agrippa with him back to Galilee. Tiberius makes Pilate's promotion official and leaves the city; he takes Caligula with him, who is furious at having to leave Agrippa. Agrippa catches Joanna praying to Jesus and reports her to Antipas. Her husband, Chuza, persuades Antipas that Joanna is insane, and she escapes punishment.

In Damascus, Saul is healed by Ananias, who was sent by Jesus to instruct Saul to take his message to the Gentiles, their kings, and the people of Israel. Saul's men don't know what has happened to their leader, but they are increasingly angered by his apparent

DID YOU KNOW?

Caligula: The emperor of Rome from AD 37 to 41, Caligula followed the reign of Tiberius. His reign was short and ended with his assassination. Caligula's behavior is often attributed to madness, as he stirred up violent riots, sanctioned persecution against Jews, and attempted to elevate himself to the level of a god. He also advanced the rule of his friend Herod Agrippa in Palestine. Caligula's short reign was followed by the appointment of the emperor Claudius.

conversion. Reuben rides fast to Jerusalem.

Claudia's dream turns prophetic. Tiberius is killed in his bed by Caligula, and Caligula is now emperor. Pilate's promotion is gone. Claudia fears worse is to come.

In Damascus, Saul ignores Barnabas's warning and preaches in the synagogue that Jesus is the Son of God. The people are enraged. Meanwhile, Reuben arrives from Damascus to tell Caiaphas that Saul too has gone over to the other side.

READ

Acts 9:1–22

KEY VERSE

"Immediately, something like scales fell from Saul's eyes, and he could see again. He got up and was baptized." —Acts 9:18

REFLECT

Have you ever followed a workout or weight loss program? There's a good chance you took a picture of yourself before you started and once you were done. Those photos can serve as a great tool to measure success.

But our culture is a little too obsessed with the before and after shots. Take a look around the Internet. They're everywhere. And come on, you've got to question how much Photoshop was used on the extreme shots that advertisers use to try to get us to sign up, join, or otherwise fork over some money to transform our bodies to look just like that.

But those advertisers know what they're doing. They know we love dramatic transformation. All the sweat and discipline and hard work in the process? See, that's just the thing. They don't want us to focus on that part. Honestly, we don't either. We want the immediate transformation—so we can skip over the long, hard process.

PAUL'S JOURNEY

When it comes to the apostle Paul, it's easy to skip over the middle. Saul's surrender is undeniably sudden and dramatic. His transformation is truly miraculous. And his story of ruthless persecutor to spiritual champion is inspirational. But even Saul had to walk a journey to become Paul.

We first encountered Saul watching Stephen's execution (Acts 8:1). At that point, Saul had observed the rapid spread of Christianity. He then witnessed Stephen's peace and forgiveness of his murderers at his death. And as Saul began persecuting Christians, he watched time after time as the people he threatened and abused went right back to preaching and worshipping. The more Saul saw the power of what these people had, the more he sought to destroy it. He was not fighting against something human, but against the supernatural power of God in the lives of His people.

DID YOU KNOW?

Damascus: A thriving city about 150 miles from Jerusalem, Damascus had a large population of Jews, a strong Greek influence, and Roman rule. The city was located between the fertile belt and the Arabian desert, making it the center of extensive trade that stretched into Mesopotamia, Syria, Anatolia, Persia, and Arabia. That's probably why Saul was especially intent on stopping the spread of Christianity here. Any ideas or beliefs that thrived in the city of Damascus would soon spread to the many locations impacted by the trade routes.

So when we see Saul on the road to Damascus in Acts 9:1–2, he's not headed there on vacation. Damascus was a four- to six-day journey from Jerusalem on foot. That's a lot of walking. But in his obsession to destroy Christianity, Saul had obtained the right to bring Christians who had escaped to Damascus back to Jerusalem. Once back in Jerusalem, the full power of the Sanhedrin could be leveraged to try them and put them to death.

But things didn't go as Saul planned. Instead, he encountered God—who had other plans. God's intervention in Saul's life was undeniable. There was bright light, God's voice spoke, and Saul was blinded. What had to be most shocking for Saul, though, were the words he heard. The conversation went like this:

"Saul, Saul, why do you persecute me?"

"Who are you, Lord?" Saul asked.

"I am Jesus, whom you are persecuting," he replied. "Now get up and go into the city, and you will be told what you must do" (Acts 9:4–6).

But that point still wasn't the fullness of his conversion. Saul had to choose to obey and do as he was told. This wasn't necessarily an easy task for someone completely devoted to doing the exact opposite of what he had been instructed. Can you imagine the rest of Saul's walk to Damascus? What was going through his mind as his companions led him, blind, along the rocky road? Acts 9:9 is easy to overlook but says a lot: "He remained there blind for three days and did not eat or drink" (NLT).

Those three days must have felt like an eternity. It was as if Saul was in a tomb of his own for three days. In the darkness, was he fasting by choice or was he too awestruck to eat after his encounter with Jesus? Was he sunken into confusion about this unexpected discovery that would upend his entire life? Was he wracked with guilt about the pain and evil he had unleashed at the Messiah Himself? Undoubtedly, Saul was undone.

It was Ananias whom God used to heal, restore, and bring the gift of the Holy Spirit to Saul. And then we see Saul surrender and be baptized.

Ananias also had to make a choice about how to respond to God. In a vision, God told Ananias to go to a certain house and ask for Saul of Tarsus. "Um, are you sure, God? I don't think that's such a good idea," Ananias essentially said first. "You do know that Saul is the guy who is terrorizing us down here, don't you?"

But God said to go, and Ananias was obedient. He went and greeted the man as "Brother Saul" (Acts 9:17). And Ananias surrendered to the power of God through him to heal Saul and fill him with the Holy Spirit.

The conversion of Paul—as he later became better known—is the most famous conversion story in history. It's amazing not just because of its visions and miracles, but because of the radical change in Paul—and how that demonstrates the power of God's forgiveness. God chose the man who had been the most evil and destructive toward the believers to be His "chosen instrument to proclaim my name to the Gentiles and their kings and to the people of Israel" (Acts 9:15). Paul went from worst enemy to prime representative. If God can choose and change Paul, He can do the same for any of us in any area of our lives.

It's tempting to take the "after" photo of Saul right then. It certainly would have shown an extreme difference. But really, Saul's journey was just getting started. He would go on to travel and preach and suffer greatly for the Gospel. He did not have an easy road. In Philippians 1:12–14, he recounted the many things he had suffered. There must have been many days and nights while Paul lay chained or beaten or bleeding that he remembered hearing the voice of Jesus on that road to Damascus.

Our response to Christ's calling won't mean the end of difficulty for us either. But like Paul must have done, we can draw encouragement from the memory of our first awareness of Jesus's call. And we can trust our ultimate purpose and destination to Him.

APPLY

We may not be in the place of Saul, an active opponent of the Gospel. But most of us have places in our hearts or lives that are far from God. Those areas may be fed by years of fear, anger, unforgiveness, greed, control, or rebellion. Maybe we are working contrary to God out of a sense of love—but love accompanied by a feeling that we must work to control and protect those we love. In those areas of our lives, we are like Saul, walking down a road with our own agenda. So what should our response look like when God meets us on the journey?

1. Pay attention.

When you sense God calling for your attention or speaking to you through His Word, other people, or other means, acknowledge Him. Don't look the other way or occupy yourself with distractions. Give Him your attention and trust that He will make the next step clear, just as He did for Saul (Isaiah 30:21).

2. Obey.

Do what He says—even if doesn't make sense. God told Saul to go into the city, where he would be told what to do. Sometimes our obedience is simply to do something that God asks. That guidance begins in God's Word and flows out of it. We may not always understand the ultimate purpose, or it may become clear in due time. But as we obey, we grow in our understanding of God's heart (John 14:15).

3. Surrender.

Our spiritual response is to give up our resistance, control, or disagreement—to trade them for trust in action by choosing to obey God. Surrendering to God opens us to His work in our lives. This begins with our surrender to His offer of forgiveness and eternal life (Romans 6:23; 10:9–10). It continues in our daily lives as we learn to listen to and trust the Holy Spirit's leading (John 10:27; Proverbs 3:5–6).

DISCUSS

Describe a time when God confronted you on your life journey. How did you respond? What was the result?

Not many of us experience blinding light and God's audible voice. What are some ways God uses to get our attention and speak to us?

Is God asking you to be part of someone else's journey and surrender? What's your response?

Have you chosen to believe in Jesus and place your life in His hands? Why or why not?

Read and discuss the following verses. What do they tell you about God's calling and our response?

"For it is by grace you have been saved, through faith—and this is not from yourselves, it is the gift of God—not by works, so that no one can boast." —Ephesians 2:8–9

"Here I am! I stand at the door and knock. If anyone hears my voice and opens the door, I will come in and eat with that person, and they with me." —Revelation 3:20

"Whoever has my commands and keeps them is the one who loves me. The one who loves me will be loved by my Father, and I too will love them and show myself to them." —John 14:21

"He will call on me, and I will answer him; I will be with him in trouble, I will deliver him and honor him." —Psalm 91:15

"Therefore, I urge you, brothers and sisters, in view of God's mercy, to offer your bodies as a living sacrifice, holy and pleasing to God—this is your true and proper worship. Do not conform to the pattern of this world, but be transformed by the renewing of your mind. Then you will be able to test and approve what God's will is—his good, pleasing and perfect will." —Romans 12:1–2

PRAY

Heavenly Father, reveal where we are far from you. Intercept us in our ignorance or disobedience. Lead us down your roads for your purposes, and give us the strength and courage to listen, obey, and surrender to you. Our journey is yours to guide.

ACT

Find a labyrinth in your area and set aside time to walk through it. If one is not available, find a garden path or a park trail that allows you to walk without interruption. Walking is proven to increase creative thinking, and it gives you a chance to block out other life distractions and focus on what God wants to communicate to you. Ask God to speak. Meditate on a Bible verse as you walk, and use the time to actively listen.

LESSON

LET IT GO

REVIEW: EPISODE 9

Barnabas helps Saul escape from the angry Jews in Damascus by lowering him in a basket down the city walls.

Leah suggests killing the traitor Saul, but Caiaphas prefers trying to convert him back into the temple fold. Caiaphas orders Reuben to find Saul.

When they arrive back in Jerusalem, Barnabas brokers a meeting between Saul and the disciples, but they are not happy to see him again.

Caligula is determined to assert his power. He tells Pilate that a huge statue of himself, Emperor Caligula, will be placed in the temple. Pilate knows this will cause riot, rebellion, and war among the people, but he is powerless to speak out against it. Before Caligula leaves, Mary manages to save a young servant girl, Tabitha, from his advances.

Saul finally meets with Peter, and they discuss Jesus and their faith. Though they do not initially get along, Peter agrees to welcome Saul into the church—aided by Barnabas vouching for Saul.

Pilate informs Caiaphas and Antipas of the statue. The Jewish men are irate. They urge him to stop the statue's arrival, even though they all realize it is unstoppable. Pilate and Cornelius begin to plan for a full-scale riot. Leah proposes that Herodias and Claudia should target Saul and the Christians in an attempt to appease Caligula. Herodias is in favor, but Claudia is appalled.

Antipas and Herodias decide that the statue brings political opportunities, so they stay to take advantage of the fallout. Mary overhears their conversation and learns of the statue. She anticipates Jesus's prophesied end of days and rushes to inform the disciples, with money from Joanna to support her. Chuza is furious when he discovers that Joanna has given their money for her secret faith.

Tabitha witnesses their discussion and likes what she hears about this message of Jesus.

Simon is frustrated when the others don't rush into action to stop the statue from desecrating the temple, so he goes to the zealots.

Saul is captured and imprisoned by Reuben. Caiaphas wants to see him.

READ

Acts 9:22–29

KEY VERSE

"When [Saul] came to Jerusalem, he tried to join the disciples, but they were all afraid of him, not believing that he really was a disciple." —Acts 9:26

REFLECT

We've all had that dreaded moment of walking down the aisle in any given store when suddenly we hear our name—with just a bit of question to it, like the person is trying to sound unsure that it's us but really they know exactly that it's us.

You'd know that voice anywhere, without even needing to turn around. It's the boss with a bad temper who fired you, or the ex-boyfriend/girlfriend who cheated on you, or the friend you fought with two years ago and haven't spoken to since, or the ex-husband/wife—or worse, the ex-husband/wife's mother. Whoever the person is specifically, there's only one word to describe the encounter: *awkward*.

You might stand and make small talk for a few minutes. You try to put on a good face—to sound like you're doing great. But inside you feel old wounds festering, and you can't wait to get away as soon as possible.

ARE YOU FOR REAL?

Saul must have had a lot of awkward encounters after meeting Jesus on the road to Damascus—unless people saw him first and were able to avoid him altogether. That's what most of the Christians wanted to do.

Saul's salvation and forgiveness were complete the moment he surrendered to God, but the journey wasn't over. Saul had to live with the reputation he had built and the consequences of how he had treated people. Starting in Damascus, he had to answer the skeptics by proving things were different. Words weren't enough. Saul had done more damage to Christians than anyone else around. And if you're trying to hunt down believers to arrest and kill them, what's the best way? Say you're a believer, get them to come to you, then *wham*, lower the trap. Oldest trick in the book. Nobody wanted to come running to meet Saul just because he said he'd had a change of heart.

But Saul immediately began preaching, and people who started out skeptical were amazed. He continued proving his life had been changed through Jesus, the Messiah. But that took awhile. Acts 9:23 says, "After many days had gone by . . ." But Paul's own account in Galatians 1 gives a time line of about three years before he left Damascus.

Damascus was only the beginning. From there Saul went on a journey through his past, each step taking him to a place of increasing past reputation. In Damascus he was known and feared, but he had less personal history to deal with. Then he returned to Jerusalem, the center of his brutal campaign against Christians. Finally, he went back to his native home, Tarsus, where he would again have to prove that he was not the man he used to be.

In Jerusalem, Saul's reputation was widespread, and the disciples didn't want anything to do with him. Acts 9:26 says, "When he came to Jerusalem, he tried to join the disciples, but they were all afraid of him, not believing that he really was a disciple." Who could blame them? They still didn't trust the guy who had wanted to murder them. Understandably, they still felt fear and probably anger and resentment toward him. Naturally, it would have been hard to believe Saul had changed.

Barnabas was different. He literally put his neck on the line and showed a contrast among the disciples. Barnabas stood up for Saul and acted as a bridge between the old and the new. His willingness to meet Saul demonstrated his confidence that the power they preached in Jesus was truly enough to change even the greatest sinner. In Barnabas we see hope, forgiveness, and freedom. He was willing to see the best in Saul—and in God's power to transform the worst of humanity.

DID YOU KNOW?

Tarsus: Saul's hometown was an important stop for traders and was a learning center of the ancient world, alongside Alexandria and Athens. The city lies in south-central Turkey, about twelve miles inland from the Mediterranean Sea. During Saul's time, Jewish citizens of Tarsus were granted Roman citizenship. The biblical mention of Paul as a tentmaker (Acts 18:3) fits well with the city's reputation for producing a certain type of felt cloth from the wool of shaggy black goats. The modern city of Cumhuriyet Alani sits above the ruins of the ancient city, so little of Tarsus during the time of Paul has been excavated.

APPLY

It's natural to be skeptical of people. When they've built a strong reputation by one type of actions, it's hard to trust them when they claim the opposite. Even when God does a powerful work in their lives, it can take time for us to get over the hurts they've caused us and to fully trust that they won't hurt us so badly again. So what does it look like to step back and accept God's work in our own lives and the lives of others?

1. Forgive yourself.

If you confess your sin to God, you are forgiven. It's a done deal (1 John 1:9). But the process of moving past the repercussions of sin can take longer. And letting go of our guilt in order to forgive ourselves can be tough. It's often a continual process because history on earth doesn't get erased even though our sin is removed. We may still live with consequences, reputation, and guilt.

Satan loves this. He is our accuser (Revelation 12:10), and he loves to drag up what once was and accuse us over and over again. As we walk the path of change, we have to hold tight to the promise that the old has gone and the new has come. Memorizing verses that remind us of this can help when doubt and guilt surface. Start with these:

"Therefore, if anyone is in Christ, the new creation has come: The old has gone, the new is here!" —2 Corinthians 5:17

"I have been crucified with Christ and I no longer live, but Christ lives in me. The life I now live in the body, I live by faith in the Son of God, who loved me and gave himself for me." —Galatians 2:20

2. Believe the best about others.

If we're honest, sometimes we find satisfaction in holding onto the sin of others. It keeps them in a box and justifies our own feelings and reactions toward them. But our blame and bitterness only destroy us from the inside. When we open our hearts and look for the best in others, we acknowledge that the same grace and forgiveness given to us is also at work in others. God's forgiveness and power are bigger than us! So when you are tempted to hold onto the bad you've seen in someone, make the conscious choice to look for the good. Give others space to change, improve, and grow. If there is doubt, reach out and see for yourself instead of hiding behind rumors. Be like Barnabas and take a stand for believing the best about others (Colossians 3:13).

3. Know the difference between discernment and judgment.

Even in forgiveness, there is still room for caution, wisdom, and accountability. A spouse returning to an abusive relationship over and over because she wants to believe the best about her abuser is not the right thing. There are those who use grace as an excuse to continue sinning. We should be wary of them and not be fooled. God can heal and change even an abuser, but He usually uses a network of other people to help heal deep hurts, change lifelong patterns, and protect victims from more harm.

So how can we be trusting but not naive? The key lies in the proof. Saul continually proved through his actions that the change in his life was real. Test, listen, and observe. Pray for wisdom and seek the input of others. In this way, you can pursue discernment without judgment (Philippians 1:9–11).

DISCUSS

What are you known for that you wish you could erase? How have you been judged by others for your past?

Who do you need to forgive? How can you actively pursue reconciliation and acceptance of them as the person they are today through Christ?

Is there someone in your life who needs you to be a Barnabas? How can you stand up for them and speak the truth of the transformation God has brought in their life?

How can you support someone you know by helping them seek discernment without judgment?

Read and discuss the following verses. What do they tell you about letting go of judgment and placing it in God's hands?

> "There is only one Lawgiver and Judge, the one who is able to save and destroy. But you—who are you to judge your neighbor?" —James 4:12

> "Therefore judge nothing before the appointed time; wait until the Lord comes. He will bring to light what is hidden in darkness and will expose the motives of the heart. At that time each will receive their praise from God." —1 Corinthians 4:5

> "If it is possible, as far as it depends on you, live at peace with everyone. Do not take revenge, my dear friends, but leave room for God's wrath, for it is written: 'It is mine to avenge; I will repay,' says the Lord. On the contrary: 'If your enemy is hungry, feed him; if he is thirsty, give him something to drink. In doing this, you will heap burning coals on his head.' Do not be overcome by evil, but overcome evil with good." —Romans 12:18–21

> "Therefore, as God's chosen people, holy and dearly loved, clothe yourselves with compassion, kindness, humility, gentleness and patience. Bear with each other and forgive one another

if any of you has a grievance against someone. Forgive as the Lord forgave you. And over all these virtues put on love, which binds them all together in perfect unity. Let the peace of Christ rule in your hearts, since as members of one body you were called to peace. And be thankful." —Colossians 3:12–15

"Do not conform to the pattern of this world, but be transformed by the renewing of your mind. Then you will be able to test and approve what God's will is—his good, pleasing and perfect will." —Romans 12:2

PRAY

God, thank you that you don't treat us like we treat each other. Please open our eyes to see where we unfairly judge others by human standards. Shape our hearts and give us wisdom and discernment to see and understand life like you do. Give us grace to forgive, love to accept, and patience to let you do your work in our hearts and the hearts of others.

ACT

Choose to forgive. Let someone off the hook of your resentment. Let go of your anger and blame for them. And make it real. Now is the time to meet face-to-face and tell them you forgive them. Start by writing what you will say and reading it aloud to yourself. When the time comes, read your letter to them if that's all you can muster. If it's physically impossible to meet face-to-face (maybe due to distance or death), mail your letter or face a chair and pretend the person is sitting there. Let go of the past and be free.

LESSON

LIFE MOMENTS

REVIEW: EPISODE 10

Jesus appears to James in His resurrected form. James's belief is reignited, and he returns to Jerusalem. Peter and the disciples realize they must ask Caiaphas for Saul's release.

Caiaphas tries speaking with Saul but is unable to sway him. He appeals to forgiveness, but Saul wants forgiveness only from Jesus for the crimes he has committed against His followers. Leah sees her husband's decision to release Saul as weak and angrily forms a different plan.

Cornelius spots Gabra the Ethiopian eunuch arriving in Jerusalem with a retinue of guards. He informs Pilate, who suspects terrorist activities. Claudia suggests inviting Gabra to dinner, where they can gauge his intentions. Cornelius delivers the invitation, just as the Ethiopian is giving a large donation to the temple. Caiaphas in return gives him a precious scroll of Isaiah.

Saul ignores Caiaphas's warnings and the disciples' advice and continues to cause division with his bold words. Meanwhile, James and Caiaphas make peace. In return for safety from future arrests, Caiaphas asks the disciples to keep Saul under control. Peter and the other disciples are mixed in their reaction.

Leah strikes up her own deal with the zealots. She promises to be their spy inside the temple if Levi will get rid of Saul.

Herodias and Claudia walk in on Joanna promising to get Tabitha baptized soon. Claudia persuades Herodias to fire them rather than inflict a worse punishment. But it has come at a bad time. Gabra is present for dinner, and he and Pilate hear of the Christians in the palace. Pilate wants to make an example in front of Gabra, so he has Tabitha flogged and Joanna imprisoned.

Claudia enables the escape of Mary and badly beaten Tabitha, and they return to the disciples.

Later, Gabra meets with Levi to discuss arming the Jewish people with weapons, ready for war should the statue of Caligula enter the temple.

It's clear that Saul and James won't agree on various issues. Saul keeps preaching brazenly in a hostile city. He will not be deterred from his quest to atone for his sins. But it's too dangerous for Saul to be in Jerusalem, so the disciples take him out of the city and send him off to Tarsus.

READ

Acts 8:26–40; 9:20–25

KEY VERSES

"'How can I [understand],' he said, 'unless someone explains it to me?' So he invited Philip to come up and sit with him....Then Philip began with that very passage of Scripture and told him the good news about Jesus."
—Acts 8:31, 35

DID YOU KNOW?

Eunuch: The primary definition is a male who has been intentionally castrated. However, the term can also refer to a man with a birth defect or other medical issue that causes impotence, or may simply be a title for someone who voluntarily chooses to forgo marriage and sexual relations in order to serve the Lord in some capacity. It was a common practice in ancient times for rulers to castrate some servants, especially those who attended royalty or held certain offices. Acts 8:27 tells us that the Ethiopian eunuch fit this description as "an important official in charge of all the treasury of the Kandake (which means 'queen of the Ethiopians')."

REFLECT

Don't you hate getting interrupted? We live busy lives. Most of us have our days scheduled out and filled up with demands from work, school, church, and extracurriculars. Our bosses want reports. Our teachers want assignments. Our coaches want practice. Our bills need to be paid.

Our homes and cars need repairs. Our kids want to play. We have important stuff going on here, people!

So don't you hate it when you're right in the middle of something important—and the phone rings, the dog yelps in pain, or your daughter tugs on your sleeve. Sometimes those interruptions are frustrating distractions. But any parent knows that a child's call often results in a meaningful moment—of course, sometimes not. We can never quite tell beforehand.

Sometimes God calls us from what we think is important and asks us to do something mundane. We might even view it as an annoying distraction. But in God's economy, the ordinary is often the path that leads to something more important than we can see or know. His work in the ordinary can be extraordinary.

That's what Philip discovered.

GO WHERE?

Philip had groundbreaking ministry going on in Samaria. He was on the cutting edge of spreading the Gospel to a new people group and seeing it heal centuries-

DID YOU KNOW?

Baptism: The ritual of immersing oneself in water for cleansing dates back to the Old Testament. And many religions and cults of Jesus's day incorporated ceremonial baths as a form of cleansing. These were usually in pools of water large enough for immersion but sometimes used only a ceremonial sprinkling of water. The baptism that John the Baptist performed was related to repentance and the forgiveness of sin, but was not specifically connected to faith in Jesus. So the foundation of what we know today as Christian baptism was laid by the baptism of Jesus Himself. When John baptized Him, Jesus was acknowledged as the Son of God (Mark 1:11) and received the Holy Spirit (Mark 1:10). The practice of baptism in the early church was immediate baptism on acceptance of the Gospel message. Later, baptism was often preceded by a time of instruction, prayer, or fasting.

DID YOU KNOW?

Ethiopia: The Ethiopia of Philip's time wasn't the exact nation we know today, but it was close. The ancient Ethiopian kingdom was the kingdom of Meroe, which covered from the Upper Nile region south to Khartoum, where the Blue and White Nile Rivers converged. The name Kandake or Candace that we see mentioned in our Bible translations was the title of the queen, not her actual name.

old wounds. As a leader in this spiritual movement, Philip would have had many demands and responsibilities. Sick people would have wanted to be healed. Hurting people would have wanted to hear the life-giving message. There is no doubt God was using Philip in powerful ways.

And then God told Philip to go take a walk in the desert. That must have sounded like an unusual request. Sure, it was delivered by an angel, but it still must have seemed like an awfully ordinary task—maybe even an annoying distraction. It would have been easy for Philip to say he had more important things to do than go wait by the side of a road.

But Philip obeyed. And out there in the middle of the wilderness, Philip encountered an Ethiopian official—who was reading the prophet Isaiah and wanting to understand what it meant. Philip was in exactly the right place at exactly the right moment. He was able to explain the message of Jesus to a man eager to hear.

The seemingly ordinary task that Philip was directed to do turned into a very big deal. It was obviously a big deal in the life of the Ethiopian who believed and was baptized. And although the Bible doesn't specifically say, it is generally believed that this official in the queen's court was then responsible for carrying the message of Jesus back to his country on the continent of Africa.

Philip's willingness to step away from what seemed like the most important in order to be present in the ordinary created an opportunity for the boundaries of the Gospel to spread farther around the world.

It seems to be one of God's favorite ways to work, doesn't it? Using the plain, humble, and absolutely ordinary to reveal and accomplish the extraordinary. How about these examples? A leader who's afraid of public speaking to deliver the people from slavery. A boy king to defeat a giant with a slingshot. A Messiah born in an animal stall. God Himself in the trappings of a human. The salvation of the world through a criminal's execution. And a ragtag bunch of social and spiritual nobodies to be His messengers to the world.

That's good news for all the rest of us.

APPLY

God clearly values availability over ability. And He wants to use us in and through everyday events. That doesn't mean He won't call us more specifically to some larger task. But God sees the events of our lives differently than we do. Everything is significant. Every act and appointment is coated with spiritual expression and eternal resonance. As God's people on earth, we carry His message in and through everything we do. We reflect His light all around us, whether we are changing diapers, writing software code, or studying calculus. What we see as common, God sees as part of a much more significant process. And in those ordinary moments, He may meet us and use us for unexpected or unseen purposes. At the same time, what we consider the most engaging and meaningful may not always be the most important to Him. So how can we shift our perspective and show up for God in the ordinary moments of life?

1. Be attentive.
The flow of our world runs contrary to God's. It clambers for our time and shouts for our attention. And we must consciously tune our ears to hear God's quiet voice (1 Kings 19:11–13). In our busy lives, we must be disciplined to build in time to listen. As we do, we make ourselves available to hear the Holy Spirit's guidance and see through the distractions to recognize the significance of even seemingly small events. The more we develop God's perspective, the more we understand His work in and around us (1 Corinthians 2:14).

2. Be available.
Wherever you find yourself, be all there. Philip went out on a desert road. Then he ran alongside a chariot. Then he asked a question: "Hey, what are you reading? Do you understand it?" The Holy Spirit

gave Philip guidance one step at a time. But Philip had to show up and be willing to take each step. Sometimes just being present and asking questions of others opens the door for us to connect and be part of God's work in their lives—and ours.

3. Be humble.

Philip could have easily considered himself too important to go hang out on a dusty road. We may think we're too important or too in charge to do the menial task. Sure, there's a place for delegation, but sometimes God calls us out to the seemingly lowly jobs (Philippians 2:3–5; James 4:10). And like Philip, when we serve others with humility, we get to be part of God's important work.

DISCUSS

What are the mundane activities of your life? Do you enjoy or despise them?

Have you ever felt God calling you away from an important task, a thriving ministry, a flourishing career, or an exciting adventure and asking you to do something more ordinary, even boring? Describe.

How have you seen God work in and through you in those everyday, regular moments?

Describe a time when God turned your ordinary into something extraordinary for His kingdom.

Read and discuss the following verses. What do they tell you about the importance of our faithfulness in the ordinary moments of life?

> "He replied, 'Blessed rather are those who hear the word of God and obey it.'" —Luke 11:28

> "Remind the people to be subject to rulers and authorities, to be obedient, to be ready to do whatever is good, to slander no one, to be peaceable and considerate, and always to be gentle toward everyone." —Titus 3:1–2

> "By faith Abraham, when called to go to a place he would later receive as his inheritance, obeyed and went, even though he did not know where he was going. By faith he made his home

in the promised land like a stranger in a foreign country; he lived in tents, as did Isaac and Jacob, who were heirs with him of the same promise. For he was looking forward to the city with foundations, whose architect and builder is God." —Hebrews 11:8–10

"Therefore, since we are surrounded by such a great cloud of witnesses, let us throw off everything that hinders and the sin that so easily entangles. And let us run with perseverance the race marked out for us, fixing our eyes on Jesus, the pioneer and perfecter of faith. For the joy set before him he endured the cross, scorning its shame, and sat down at the right hand of the throne of God. Consider him who endured such opposition from sinners, so that you will not grow weary and lose heart." —Hebrews 12:1–3

"Whatever you do, work at it with all your heart, as working for the Lord, not for human masters, since you know that you will receive an inheritance from the Lord as a reward. It is the Lord Christ you are serving." —Colossians 3:23–24

PRAY

Lord, reveal where we are complacent or even frustrated in the everyday tasks of our lives. Please realign our vision. Give us your eyes to see what you are up to around us and your ears to hear the Spirit's guidance. Give us your strength and discipline to make hard choices about our schedules and priorities. And make us alert to your calling in the midst of our ordinary moments.

ACT

What's the most mundane task you can think of? Cleaning the house? Mowing the yard? Choose a common task and do it. But head into your boring job with a different, prayerful perspective. Ask God to meet you in the midst of it. Focus on Colossians 3:23–24 throughout the process. Worship God with song and with your actions. See what God will do in and through you.

LESSON
11

CREDIT THE SOURCE

REVIEW: EPISODE 11

James the Just steps into more leadership among the Christians as he negotiates peace with Caiaphas. Caiaphas promises an end to arrests, and Leah is predictably furious with her husband for striking such a deal. She starts to wonder if he is fit for the job any longer.

More zealots arrive in the city to rally around Levi, and Pilate becomes increasingly paranoid about the threat posed by Gabra, the Ethiopian eunuch. Indeed, Gabra is meeting with Levi to support the Jewish cause against the Romans.

There is growing friction between Peter and James the Just over the way to lead the group of believers through the impending statue crisis. Some of the disciples wonder if this is the end of days and the signs that Jesus spoke about. The debate causes everyone to consider his or her personal calling. Peter needs to reset the purpose of his mission, so he leaves Jerusalem for the rural areas he began his work in.

Claudia tries to secure the release of the imprisoned Joanna, but Pilate is unmoved. Cornelius watches and finds himself increasingly drawn to Claudia's faith. Joanna tells Mary to take Tabitha back home to Joppa, where she can be with her family.

Peter meets up with Philip in Samaria. Philip is visited by the Holy Spirit, who tells him to go out on the desert road.

Peter continues on to Joppa. When he arrives, Mary is there, and she delivers the distressing news that Tabitha has died. Peter finds himself at a personally low moment, doubting his abilities to lead the church, but it's then that he achieves the greatest miracle: bringing Tabitha back to life.

Caiaphas meets Gabra, who denies any alliance with Levi. But Leah double-crosses her husband and goes to Pilate with information on the alliance. Many are arrested, and Gabra is evicted from Jerusalem in humiliating fashion.

Claudia tries to free Joanna behind Pilate's back. But Pilate stops her. He ramps up the punishment of Joanna and orders her immediate execution. Cornelius is tasked with the execution, which he loathes. Afterward, he weeps bitterly and leaves the city to return to his family.

Philip passes Gabra on the desert road. The Ethiopian is reading Isaiah's scroll, and Philip helps him make sense of it. Gabra hears and believes the Gospel, and he is baptized.

Just when Pilate has rid the city of rebels, he gets terrible news: the statue has arrived.

READ

Acts 9:32–43

KEY VERSE

"This became known all over Joppa, and many people believed in the Lord." —Acts 9:42

REFLECT

Have you ever accidentally been credited for something you didn't do? Maybe it happened in school, when a teacher assumed an assignment or project was yours. Maybe it was at work, when the boss called you out for a job well done—that you had little to do with. Maybe a friend or neighbor jumped to the conclusion that a good deed must have come from you.

Did you correct them? Did you set the record straight? Did you conveniently just let it slide? *Hey, I never said I did it; nothing wrong if they want to believe that.* Or did you jump on the chance to make yourself look good? *Why, yes. Yes, I did do that awesome act; it was all me.*

Do you remember the '80s pop group Milli Vanilli? If not, here's a lesson in musical infamy and in taking credit. The duo scored several No. 1 hits and won a Grammy for best new artist in 1990. But their success unraveled the same year when it was discovered that the two hadn't sung a note of their music. The two "singers" were actually a pair of models and dancers who lip-synched their way through videos and performances. The record's producer didn't think the original singers were marketable enough, so he hired some eye candy. It worked—for a while—selling fourteen million albums. Even when the news began to go public, the fake Milli Vanilli tried to defend themselves and keep taking credit for the music. But it didn't take long for their career to fizzle completely. Even the Grammy was taken back.

Eventually the truth will come out. One way or the other, true credit will be given where it is due.

IT WASN'T ME

Acts 9 tells two stories about the impact of Peter's ministry. The first story is about Aeneas, a man who had been paralyzed and bedridden for eight years. Peter healed him, but he didn't say, "I heal you." Instead, Peter clearly said, "Jesus Christ heals you" (Acts 9:34). The text says all those who lived in Lydda and the neighboring village of Sharon believed in Jesus because of this miracle. The man's illness had lasted a long time—long

DID YOU KNOW?

Lydda: A smaller town about twelve miles from Joppa. It was located at the intersection of the main roads between Egypt and Syria, and Jerusalem and Joppa.

DID YOU KNOW?

Sharon: The fertile plain of Sharon is the most common area referenced by this name. It is a region that runs fifty miles along the Mediterranean coast. But the reference in this passage of Acts more likely refers instead to a village near Lydda.

enough that everyone knew about it. So when Aeneas was back on his feet, out in the village walking around again, word spread fast.

In the second story, Peter raised a woman named Tabitha from the dead in Joppa. Again, the simplicity of the telling of the story shows us that Peter did not make a spectacle of the event. He sent Tabitha's friends and mourners away, prayed, and then told Tabitha to get up. It was truly amazing! Peter brought a dead person back to life! Even he must have been impressed—but not with himself, with the power of the Holy Spirit.

Peter clearly did not perform these acts to gain personal followers or to bring honor to himself. The text doesn't say that people believed in or followed Peter. Rather, many people believed in Jesus. That's what Peter had in mind all along.

Peter's work and attitude are a stark contrast to Simon the Sorcerer, who we read about in Acts 8. Simon amazed people with miracles and sorcery, but his purpose was to bring attention and money to himself. We are told that Simon boasted to the people that he was something great. Peter simply pointed people to the source of his power.

Can you imagine the chaos if every apostle started taking personal credit for the signs and miracles they performed? It would have quickly become a miracle-working competition, without any eternal value. Instead, as they gave the credit to God, many believed in Jesus as the Messiah and had their lives transformed.

The struggle for all of us, of course, is that the temptation for attention, praise, and prestige is strong. We often feel an

DID YOU KNOW?

Joppa: The main seaport of Judea, Joppa was about forty miles from Jerusalem and has been an important city throughout history. This is the same port Jonah came to when fleeing from the Lord (Jonah 1:3). It is also where cedars arrived and were then transported to Jerusalem to build Solomon's temple (2 Chronicles 2:16). Today, Joppa is a suburb of the modern city Tel Aviv and is known as Jaffa.

urgent need to make things happen for ourselves, and we find a deep satisfaction in taking credit for our achievements. That's not to say we shouldn't feel a sense of satisfaction for doing the right thing, giving our best effort, or succeeding at a task or goal.

The problem is that when we hold onto the credit for things we've done in the power of the Holy Spirit, the impact stops with us. There is a hollowness or emptiness. But when we give the glory to God, the ripple effect flows beyond us and points people to something much bigger and stronger. Our effectiveness in helping others to know Jesus lies in keeping our focus on Him and continually giving Him the glory.

DID YOU KNOW?

Tanner: This occupation involved treating the skins of dead animals. It was not a popular job as it required dealing with what Jewish law considered unclean. It is significant that at the end of Acts 9, Peter stays in Joppa for some time with Simon, who was a tanner. This shows Peter's growing confidence that the message of Jesus is for all people, including the Gentiles.

Giving God the credit for our successes and accomplishments requires humility and gratitude. Humility is one of those virtues that sounds really good but is tough to practice. The good news is that it also takes the pressure off us. When humility is rooted in gratitude, it comes easier. When we understand that even our skills, abilities, and opportunities are gifts that have been given to us, we can experience thankfulness that fuels humble acceptance. And when we humbly acknowledge that God is the source of everything in our lives, we no longer have to try to prove ourselves. God is proving Himself to the world through us. While hard work remains, our striving is done. Our success and worth are not tied to performance alone. It is not our work, but the work of God through us. And there is freedom in joining Him in what He is doing instead of trying to claim it for our own fame or glory.

APPLY

We live in a world that loves celebrity—and a world in which you can become famous simply for being famous. We won't name any names, but a few people probably come quickly to mind. On the other hand, you can probably think of people who are famous for their skills and abilities, but who are marked by humility and a desire to use their platform to accomplish good, maybe even to honor God.

We may not have a worldwide audience, but we don't have to. God has given each of us skills, abilities, passions, and opportunities. Whether your deeds are seen by one person or one million, you can give glory to God by keeping your focus on Him. What does this look like?

1. Give credit.

From each simple breath we take to our most amazing accomplishments, God is our source of life. And so our automatic reaction should always be thankful acknowledgment to God. We may have different ways of crediting God publically—some proclaim loudly; others set a quiet example. What's most important is our attitude and that we live it out consistently. It starts in our hearts and is expressed in our words and actions. Using our lives to reflect attention back to God gives other people the opportunity to know and follow Him (Psalm 115:1; 1 Peter 4:10–11).

2. Practice humility.

We don't have to stop doing powerful and influential things. Humility isn't about what you do, but about your attitude in doing it. Instead of letting ourselves believe we're greater than we are, humility is acknowledging God's greatness. Humility fuels the ability to put other people ahead of ourselves and to lift them up before ourselves (Philippians 2:3–4). Humility keeps our pride in check as we focus on God and others instead of ourselves. Does this mean we never enjoy the benefit of anything we do? Of course not. We can receive compliments and honors and thanks. The point is not to push those away, but to use them as opportunities to point to the One even greater than us.

3. Establish accountability.

It's tough not to get a big head. We all like praise. It's human nature to seek acceptance and recognition. But a good friend, family member, mentor, or coworker can help keep us in place. Having even one relationship with intentional accountability can help us remain humble and focused on the right things. Our part is to clearly ask that person to help us honestly assess where our priorities are and listen to their input. We can pray for and support each other with the aim of consistently giving credit and glory to God (1 Thessalonians 5:11; Proverbs 27:17).

DISCUSS

What would you like to be famous for? What would you do if you were a celebrity with worldwide recognition?

In what areas of your life do you feel most entitled to receive credit? Why is it hard to credit God for those?

If you've experienced accountability, describe the relationship and how it has helped you grow in humility.

When or how have you given credit to someone else? To God? What results did you see?

Read and discuss the following verses. What do they tell you about glorifying God?

> "For it is by grace you have been saved, through faith—and this is not from yourselves, it is the gift of God—not by works, so that no one can boast." —Ephesians 2:8–9

> "And whatever you do, whether in word or deed, do it all in the name of the Lord Jesus, giving thanks to God the Father through him." —Colossians 3:17

> "When pride comes, then comes disgrace, but with humility comes wisdom." —Proverbs 11:2

"Not to us, LORD, not to us but to your name be the glory, because of your love and faithfulness." —Psalm 115:1

"If anyone speaks, they should do so as one who speaks the very words of God. If anyone serves, they should do so with the strength God provides, so that in all things God may be praised through Jesus Christ. To him be the glory and the power for ever and ever. Amen." —1 Peter 4:11

PRAY

Lord, forgive us for trying to steal your glory. All that we have and are comes from you, and we are thankful for every good gift you give us. Teach us to live with humility. Give us wisdom and strength to always acknowledge you and to give you glory. Let our lives point to you in everything we do.

ACT

Do an anonymous good deed or act of service for someone who doesn't expect it. Better yet, leave a nameless note pointing credit toward God. Be creative in how you serve; just don't get caught in the act.

LESSON

UNSTOPPABLE

REVIEW: EPISODE 12

Cornelius has a vision telling him to send for Peter in Joppa. Peter likewise has a vision that encourages him to go with the soldiers sent by Cornelius.

Levi tells Caiaphas that someone within the temple must have betrayed them to the Romans. They come to blows about how to defend the temple against desecration by the statue of Caligula. Caiaphas states clearly that he will not fight. At the same time, Caiaphas refuses to help Pilate install the statue and promises resistance.

Peter meets with Cornelius and takes Mary along with him. Mary is unsure about converting him, but Peter knows it is the right thing to do. This is confirmed when Cornelius and his family start speaking in tongues through the power of the Holy Spirit.

Caiaphas and Leah finally split after he reveals he cannot trust her. Caiaphas meets with James the Just to ask for his support in helping stop the statue. Leah meets with Annas and Jonathan to discuss ousting her husband and installing Jonathan as the new high priest. And Levi, Simon, and Eva plot an ambush of their own against the Roman forces.

DID YOU KNOW?

Rulers of Jesus's Day: The book of Acts focuses mainly on the history of the spread of Christianity, rather than on the general and political history of the time period. But, of course, they did not happen separate from each other—and a lot happened in those early years of Christianity. It is interesting to note that within the first five years after Jesus's death and resurrection, all the rulers of the time changed. Herod was defeated by King Aretas. Pilate was dismissed. The high priest Caiaphas was replaced. And the emperor Tiberius died; Caligula replaces him as the new emperor.

Pilate intimidates Antipas into supporting the statue instal-lation, but Claudia argues with her husband over his brutality. Cornelius is ordered back to Jerusalem to assist with the statue crisis. This is a difficult task as he now returns as a Christian. Once he arrives, he invites Claudia to join the Nazarene move-ment and to find peace. She is sorely tempted.

James the Just convinces Peter and the others that they should stick by the temple and lend their support to Caiaphas. Cornelius is given the job of killing anyone who objects to the installation of the statue. But when he encounters Caiaphas and his men kneeling in submission, baring their necks, Cornelius cannot bring himself to cut down so many innocent people.

Together, they avert bloodshed—until Levi and Eva attack the Roman ranks and start a full-scale battle. Many, including Simon, Caiaphas, and Cornelius, cannot bring themselves to fight. But oth-ers can. Eva kills Leah for spreading so much poison among the Jewish people.

War has broken out in Jerusalem, and the battle forces every-one to clarify where they stand. Whose side are they on? Claudia is powerless to leave her husband to join the Christian faith, so she remains trapped in a difficult marriage. Peter concedes that James the Just has kept the group safe through his dealings with Caiaphas. The two men must learn how to lead the church together. Their sur-vival depends on it.

READ

Acts 10:1–48; 11:15–18

KEY VERSES

"Then Peter began to speak: 'I now realize how true it is that God does not show favoritism but accepts from every nation the one who fears him and does what is right. You know the message God sent to the people of Israel, announcing the good news of peace through Jesus Christ, who is Lord of all.'" —Acts 10:34–36

REFLECT

Have you ever won an argument and lost a friend?

It's easy to do. We love to be right. Sometimes we'll argue and argue and get so fixated on winning that we forget what the original argument was.

Have you been there? If so, you've probably also triumphantly made your greatest case, proven your point, put the exclamation point on your winning argument—and seen the crushing look of hurt in your opponent's eyes. Maybe that opponent was your child or your significant other or a close friend. Maybe it was even a stranger. It's at that point the victory feels awfully hollow. In that instant, the realization sinks in that there's so much more at stake than proving your point. Once the verbal weapons are lowered, the bigger picture comes back into view.

There's always a bigger picture.

SO THAT'S WHAT JESUS MEANT

As we see in this section of Acts, disagreements rose among the early Christians, even between Peter and other leaders. Fortunately, they were able to look beyond their own viewpoints to see God's.

On the surface, the story of Cornelius is pretty simple. He sees a vision, hears the message, puts his faith in Jesus, and is baptized. But on a deeper level, Cornelius's story is remarkable.

DID YOU KNOW?

Cornelius: Cornelius was a centurion, a Roman army officer theoretically in charge of a hundred men. He was part of a cohort known as the Italian Regiment, which probably consisted of Italian soldiers rather than native soldiers. They were located in Caesarea, which was thirty miles from Joppa and was the political capital of Judea under Herod and the Romans. Centurions provided stability to the Roman system and are mentioned a number of times throughout the New Testament, usually in a favorable way (Luke 7). Acts tells us that Cornelius was devout, God-fearing, and generous.

And it is extremely important to the Bible, the Church, the spread of Christianity—and most likely, to you and me. The story of Cornelius is clearly included in Acts as the opening of a whole new chapter of Christianity: salvation for all, including Gentiles.

The story begins with two visions, and it's important to note whose came first. Cornelius had a vision, and an angel instructed him to send for Peter. This is not just the story of Peter obeying God's call to go to the Gentiles—this is a story about a Gentile who was seeking God and who was obedient to Him. In fact, when the angel showed up, he relayed to Cornelius a "good job" from God: "Your prayers and gifts to the poor have come up as a memorial offering before God" (Acts 10:4).

It's also significant that Cornelius was an officer in the Roman army. To the Jews, he wasn't just a Gentile—he was the oppressor. He was the enemy they wanted to get rid of. He was exactly one of the people the Jews hoped to see the Messiah run out of town or annihilate with supernatural fury. Instead, he was the guy God was supernaturally sending to Peter.

Meanwhile, Peter had his own vision. As he prayed and sought God, a supernatural smorgasbord appeared in the sky—filled with everything the Jews had always been taught not to touch. And instead of the usual reminder to keep clean by avoiding the animals, the heavenly voice said, "Dig in!"

In true Peter form, he said what he thought without hesitation: "No way, Lord! I've never touched that stuff, and I'm not about to start now. It's off-limits. You said so!"

But God had a new message: "Do not call anything impure that God has made clean" (Acts 10:15).

Peter was getting used to some big changes in the wake of Jesus's resurrection. He was experiencing daily life filled with the power of the Holy Spirit. He was living in the midst of regular miracles and boldly spreading Jesus's message. He was learning what it looked like to follow Jesus and help others do the same. But this message still would have rocked Peter's world.

The rules and restrictions about what was clean and unclean went back as far as the Jewish people. God had given them clear laws and rules guiding all areas of life, including what they ate and how they ate it. The law shaped their whole culture of what they grew and raised and used and ate.

Do you know anyone who is vegan or who has a special diet because of food allergies? Their diet sets them apart and shapes who they are, not just physically but emotionally. It guides where they shop, what restaurants they visit or not, and how they view a menu. The Jewish diet and other laws shaped the Jews spiritually too. Their diet helped to set them apart and reminded them that they were God's people. Peter, even as a working-class fisherman, had faithfully followed Jewish dietary laws. How could God be telling him to kill and handle and prepare and eat what had always been strictly off-limits?

Peter's vision repeated three times, so maybe it took him awhile to catch on. But Peter saw the bigger picture that God was revealing. He eventually understood that the vision God was giving him wasn't only about clean and unclean animals and enjoying new cuisine—it was about the complete fulfillment of the law through Jesus. It was an important message that in Jesus, the old is gone and the new has come. And when Cornelius's messengers showed up, Peter put all the pieces together. He went to see Cornelius, and sitting in his formerly unclean house, Peter said, "You know it is against our laws for a Jewish man to enter a Gentile home like this or to associate with you. But God has shown me that I should no longer think of anyone as impure or unclean" (Acts 10:28, NLT).

Maybe it wasn't so much that Cornelius needed Peter, but that Peter and the rest of the Jewish Christians needed Cornelius in order to understand fully the truth that God's love was for all the world. Jesus's final instruction on earth must have been ringing in Peter's memory, especially that part about "to the ends of the earth" (Acts 1:8). As Cornelius accepted Peter's message about Jesus, the Holy Sprit filled him and his house. The others who had come with Peter were amazed that the Holy Spirit had been given to a Gentile (Acts 10:45). It was a clear sign that God had broken down the old barriers and opened the floodgates of salvation to all people. Peter was faithful to accept the wide reach of God's love and step aside when the unstoppable power of God showed up, even for the people he least expected.

Apparently, God wanted Peter and the rest of His followers to understand that He uses all methods necessary—visions, angels, miracles, ordinary people, and enemies—to reach all people with

His love. God's plans were and are much bigger than the limitations of our understanding. His offer is open to all humanity, and His love knows no boundaries.

That's good news for us all.

APPLY

The events and impact of the earliest believers still ripple through eternity. They have reached us and will continue on to reach others who come after us. They carry the story of connection with Jesus and the continuation of His kingdom on earth. Persecution, political upheaval, internal fighting, and human weakness cannot stop the message or the growth of the Church. God's love, Christ's life, and the gift of the Holy Spirit are for all people. And they are powerful to transform us like they have transformed believers for millennia. The questions for us are the same ones faced by the apostles and early believers: How will we respond? Where are we in God's bigger, eternal story? Seeking, resisting, willing, discovering, obeying, thriving in ministry? All of us can take several ongoing steps in response to Christ's call.

1. Seek God.
Whether you do or don't yet know Jesus personally, keep seeking. Cornelius was a God-fearer. He was not a Jew, but he sought truth with his heart and his hands. We can do those same things. They are not empty actions, but ways to open yourself to the truth of God in your life. Keep leaning in to your faith journey—God promises to meet you there (Mark 9:24; James 4:8). His offer of love, forgiveness, and life are open to all through Jesus (Romans 10:9–13).

2. Keep learning.
After being baptized, the new believers asked Peter to stay. They knew that receiving the Holy Spirit and being baptized weren't the end, but only the beginning. They were hungry to learn more. Whether you are a new believer or a lifetime follower of Jesus, there is always more to learn. Surround yourself with people who can teach you more about the endless love and grace of God. Ask those who have experienced more to share with you and challenge you as you learn what it means to follow Christ each day (Ephesians 4:11–15).

3. Get out of the way.

When Peter returned to Jerusalem, he was questioned by the other believers for his involvement with the Gentiles, but he simply gave the facts. The vision God gave, the life-changing message the Gentiles received, and the gift of the Holy Spirit to these new believers were proof enough that the unstoppable love of God for all people included Gentiles. In Acts 11:17, Peter said, "So if God gave them the same gift he gave us who believed in the Lord Jesus Christ, who was I to think that I could stand in God's way?" It didn't matter what anyone else thought about the inclusion of Gentiles in the grace of God; the fact was that they were. Sometimes we struggle with change, questions, and doubts. That's okay. But it's also important to stay rooted in God's Word, seek His wisdom to discern where God is at work beyond our current understanding, and get out of His way. We should seek to follow His leading even when our circumstances don't fully make sense to us. As we do, we will also be changed by knowing and experiencing more of the deep and wide love of God (2 Peter 3:18; Philippians 1:6; Ephesians 4:16–19).

DISCUSS

Where are you in your faith journey?

How do you feel about the statements declaring that God's grace is for all people? Despite this account of inclusion for the Gentiles, do you harbor doubts about others who might not be included?

Who do you learn from? What people or messages shape what you think and believe? Who can you seek out to help you understand what it means to live daily with Jesus?

Is there an area of your life where you need to get out of the way of the work of God's Spirit? Is there an obstacle you've been holding up that you need to release to God?

Read and discuss the following verses. What do they tell you about the unstoppable power and wide reach of salvation offered through Jesus?

"For I am not ashamed of the gospel, because it is the power of God that brings salvation to everyone who believes: first to the Jew, then to the Gentile." —Romans 1:16

"This is how God showed his love among us: He sent his one and only Son into the world that we might live through him. This is love: not that we loved God, but that he loved us and sent his Son as an atoning sacrifice for our sins." —1 John 4:9–10

"The Lord is not slow in keeping his promise, as some understand slowness. Instead he is patient with you, not wanting anyone to perish, but everyone to come to repentance." —2 Peter 3:9

"For the grace of God has appeared that offers salvation to all people. It teaches us to say 'No' to ungodliness and worldly passions, and to live self-controlled, upright and godly lives in this present age, while we wait for the blessed hope—the appearing of the glory of our great God and Savior, Jesus Christ, who gave himself for us to redeem us from all wickedness and to purify for himself a people that are his very own, eager to do what is good." —Titus 2:11–14

"Before the coming of this faith, we were held in custody under the law, locked up until the faith that was to come would be revealed. So the law was our guardian until Christ came that we might be justified by faith. Now that this faith has come, we are no longer under a guardian. So in Christ Jesus you are all children of God through faith, for all of you who were baptized into Christ have clothed yourselves with Christ. There is neither Jew nor Gentile, neither slave nor free, nor is there male and female, for you are all one in Christ Jesus." —Galatians 3:23–28

PRAY

Heavenly Father, please reveal where our view of you and your work is limited. Draw us into your ongoing story. Teach us, shape us, and use us. Fill us with your joy and abundant life, and help us to be faithful messengers of your unstoppable, wide-reaching love.

ACT

Start a spiritual conversation. Tell a friend about Jesus. Prayerfully ask God for direction and wisdom. But step out and open the door. You might start by asking questions and simply listening to your friend's spiritual perspective. As opportunity arises, be willing to share honestly about God's work in your own life. Remember, you don't have to convince your friend to accept Christ's message. Just be available, willing to speak, and ready to connect with God's bigger work in your friend's life.

LEADER'S GUIDE

LEADER'S GUIDE

KNOW THE PURPOSE

We are happy you've chosen to lead a small group study of Acts using the *Official* A.D. *Study & Guidebook*. Our hope is that you and your group members will experience the power of God in your lives in new and exciting ways through your time together in God's Word. All the information in this Leader's Guide is meant to support you as you invest in the lives of others and discover what God has to teach us all through the book of Acts and through the work of His Spirit in and among His earliest followers.

WHAT IS IT?

The *Official* A.D. *Study & Guidebook* is a twelve-lesson study based on the first ten chapters of Acts and the epic TV miniseries *A.D.*, from the world-renowned producing team of Roma Downey and Mark Burnett. Each lesson works in conjunction with an episode of the *A.D.* series. And each lesson guides you and your group through the corresponding Scripture passages and provides practical life applications. (For details on each section of the study, please see the "How to Use This Study and Guidebook" section on page 10.)

WHY DO IT?

A.D. is a groundbreaking major television network miniseries that vividly brings to life the earliest days of the Church. Millions will be watching, and people will be talking about the show, about the realistic portrayal of the spread of Jesus's message from Jerusalem to the ends of the earth, and about its relevance in our lives today.

Acts tells the story of God's work in the early church. It is the continuation of God's big story that took place with the death and resurrection of Jesus. With Jesus leaving the earth and the Holy Spirit arriving with fresh, new power, the early church was learning what it meant to live in relationship with God and how to relate to each other as more and different types of people believed. And the new believers had doubts and questions and challenges that are similar to ones we face today.

Going through this study is an excellent opportunity to learn from the early church and to have our eyes opened to God's work through the Holy Spirit in our world and lives today. And combined with the *A.D.* miniseries, it is a timely outreach tool to go deeper with people curious about God's ongoing work in the world and our lives.

PLAN AHEAD

Success in leading a small group starts with a little advance planning. Depending on the type of group you're leading, some of these items may or may not apply. But it's good to think them through and make any necessary arrangements ahead of time so that you can focus on leading people when the study begins.

CHILDCARE

If anyone from your group has children, you'll need to clarify what is (or is not) provided in the area of childcare. If possible, you can encourage people to be present at each study by providing free supervision for children. If you are meeting at church, coordinate with church leaders or youth ministry leaders to see if they can provide care. If not, hire a babysitter to watch the kids in another part of the house or in another location. If money is an issue, get creative by asking young people from your youth group or college group to volunteer time. Or maybe there are some seniors who would be willing to invest in the kids. Whatever arrangements you make, be sure the details are set and communicated to those involved in the study.

LOCATION

Choose a location that will be conducive to discussion—a place where people feel comfortable and can hear each other during discussion times. If you plan to watch *A.D.* broadcasts together, be sure you have an appropriate location with adequate equipment. Nothing fancy is needed, but make sure you have adequate space for study attendees and for children if necessary.

FOOD

Decide in advance if food will be offered during your small group times. If possible, ask someone else to handle the arrangements for food and drinks so that you can focus on leading the group. A sign-up or potluck arrangement works well and allows opportunities for involvement from the group. But it is best coordinated by someone other than the study leader.

TIMING

Each study is designed to take place in a one-hour period. Obviously, viewing the episodes and having more in-depth discussion go beyond that time frame. Based on your group's needs and desires, decide in advance whether the *A.D.* episodes will be viewed during your group time or individually.

PREPARE YOURSELF

As the leader, you set the tone for the study and for group interactions. We offer these suggestions to help make you more comfortable and effective in leading this small group study.

KNOW YOUR STUFF

You don't need to be an expert on every topic covered in Acts! And you certainly don't have to have all the answers. But it will be helpful for you to spend some time becoming familiar with the contents of this study. Read through the first ten chapters of Acts and then read through each of the lessons in this book. As an overview, the themes of the twelve lessons are:

1. **Hope for a New Beginning**—finding new hope when our dreams appear crushed

2. **Wait for It**—waiting for God to work

3. **Pentecost Power**—experiencing the power of the Holy Spirit

4. **What Matters Most**—living transparently to please God, not people

5. **A Bigger Picture**—focusing on God's bigger plans and purposes

6. **Scattered Seeds**—growing stronger in the face of trials and troubles

7. **A Wider Circle**—following Jesus to build bridges across our differences

8. **Respond to God**—surrendering to God's lead even when it's hard

9. **Let It Go**—letting God heal the past, ours and others'

10. **Life Moments**—being available to let God turn ordinary into extraordinary

11. **Credit the Source**—living and leading with humility

12. **Unstoppable**—following Jesus into our lives and beyond

KNOW YOURSELF

You are not qualified as a leader by being smarter, funnier, or holier than everyone else. A leader is simply willing to serve. But here are a few tips that will help you as you lead.

1. **Take care of yourself.** Be sure you are spending the time you need alone with God and with the people closest to you.

2. **Spend timing praying**—talking and listening to God about His purpose for this study. Ask Him for guidance and continually ask that His power be made perfect in your weakness.

3. **Know your own strengths and weaknesses,** and ask for help when you need it. Find others who are willing to support you in practical ways throughout the study.

4. **Remember that you don't have to have all the words to say.** Your main role as leader is to provide guidance and facilitate discussion among the group. Think of yourself more as a conductor than a soloist.

LEAD WELL

As the leader, you have the opportunity to cast a vision and set the tone for each meeting of your small group. From the start, share your heart for the message of Acts and the power of God in the lives of everyone present.

COMMUNICATE

Communicate with members ahead of time so they know what to expect and can come to each meeting prepared. Spend some time at the first meeting allowing everyone to share their expectations and desires for your time together. Consider making a short list of guidelines to help everyone interact well and make the most of the time you share. Set a tone of safety and respect for all members of the group to share. Be sensitive to different personality types. You can draw out quieter, more introverted members of your group by asking nonthreatening questions and addressing them directly. And talkative, extroverted members may need to be gently reminded to allow others to have a chance to participate. Be ready to use humor when needed to keep everyone on track—you may even want to establish a funny sign or signal to show when someone is off-topic or dominating the conversation. Clarifying these expectations and ground rules up front can avoid awkward or hurtful situations down the road.

COMMIT

Encourage everyone in the group to participate at the level they feel comfortable. But also challenge them to commit to the work of the study. Ask each member to commit to doing their best to be present at all the studies, to prepare for each lesson, and to contribute to the group discussions. Challenge your group to listen and speak respectfully and compassionately to all.

INVITE AND INCLUDE

The *Official* A.D. *Study & Guidebook* is intended to be used by both Christians and those who have not yet entered a relationship with Christ. This study has the power to help them experience God's amazing love for them and reflect on God's incredible work in our world and lives. Pray for God to bring to mind people you can invite to your group. Be conscious of how to make new members feel comfortable and welcome. Remember that the only knowledge of the Bible they may have is from what they have seen in *A.D.* Be patient with their questions and respectful of their opinions.

FOLLOW UP

This study provides a framework for your small group to spend twelve weeks together. During that time, it is our hope that relationships are formed, friendships are deepened, faith is strengthened, grace is shared, and hope is ignited. As the leader, you have the opportunity to create opportunities for what has been started here to continue. Whether it's regular dinners together, another small group study, a service project, or any other activity, we encourage you to follow up with the members of your group. Ask God to show you how He would have you continue to lead others for His glory.